The 21st Century PRO METHOD
JAZZ GUITAR
Swing to Bebop

by DOUG MUNRO

Alfred Music
P.O. Box 10003
Van Nuys, CA 91410-0003
alfred.com

ISBN-10: 0-7692-8931-2
ISBN-13: 978-0-7692-8931-1

Gibson Citation courtesy of Gibson Guitars

Foreword

have been involved with improvisation for as long as I can remember. As a young child, I started changing the words, melody, and rhythm of the songs I heard. My friends and family found this amusing. I was on my way to a career as an improviser and composer.

Unless you live in a vacuum, there is no such thing as a pure trial-and-error approach to learning improvisation. You watch and learn from the environment around you. Children learn through imitation. They learn to speak by imitating their parents, and then they learn to read and write. This approach of learning through imitation is what I have used as the foundation of my teaching philosophy for the past twenty years.

I designed and developed the jazz studies curriculum at The Conservatory of Music at Purchase in New York. We have had extraordinary success with our students. I feel I have refined my teaching ideas into a concise and successful approach toward improvisation. I would like to share this approach with students, players, and educators around the world. I humbly hope this book will add another brick in the great wall of existing literature on this subject.

In this book, we will explore jazz improvisation from early swing (Louis Armstrong) up to the bebop era. This book is not intended as a history book. I do feel, however, that it is important for the player to have a chronological sense of when certain approaches to jazz improvisation developed. Jazz improvisation is a musical form that is continually evolving or, sometimes, devolving. Starting from the beginnings of improvisation and working your way up to the present is a good, orderly way to build your abilities as an improvising musician.

What you are going to get in this book is a **Triple Reinforcement** approach to learning jazz improvisation. I've developed this approach during a lifetime of devotion to music: listening, playing, analyzing, transcribing, watching, teaching, learning, and always digging music. Remember: This book is not the only way to learn; it's just one way. There really is no wrong way as long as you learn. What I have tried to do here is to present some of the necessary materials in an orderly fashion with musical examples and some essential players to listen to for transcription to create a realistic method for learning. Throughout this book, you will see words that are highlighted. I have highlighted players, composers, songs, and concepts that I felt were important to emphasize. This book is filled with musical examples. The styles of many different artists are highlighted in these examples. Check these artists out, listen to them, and transcribe their solos. Transcribing is the best way to learn, in depth, about a player. I also put a lot of my own riffs and playing style in this book. When I don't attach an artist to an example, it's probably because it is one of my own. Many of the examples that I do credit the origins of still have my mark on them. After playing for more than twenty years, you can't help but develop your own voice. I hope you enjoy playing through this book as much as I enjoyed putting it together.

The Concept of Triple Reinforcement

To master a musical idea or concept, you must be able to hear it, play it, and understand it. By doing this, you are using your senses of hearing, sight, and touch as well as your powers of logic and reasoning to store the information about a single musical event. By using this approach on everything you learn, chances are you will not forget it. You will also have the ability to take abstractions of the information and use them in new and creative ways, which is essential in developing your own voice as an improviser.

Acknowledgments

This book has been a great learning experience for me. I thank God for the opportunity I've had to play and share musical ideas. There are some people I would like to acknowledge for their help, wisdom, generosity, and guidance in completing this project. I would like to thank producer Joe Ferry, who made the recommendation to Warner Bros. Publications on my behalf. To Paul Segal at DCI, who hooked me up with Aaron Stang at Warner Bros. Publications, thank you. Aaron Stang is the man most responsible for this book. He signed me to Warner Bros. Publications and has been the editor of this book. He has endured my countless e-mails, Zip disks, and phone calls, always helping me present the material in the best possible way. Aaron hipped me as to how to write this book—period. Thank you, Aaron. Marshall Toppo engineered, played on, and mixed the play-along CD that accompanies this book. I want to thank him for his endless time and dedication to completing this project. There are other people whose brains and record collections I have picked during the writing of this book. Guitarist Gil Parris has an endless record collection and total recall of every track and player; thank you for your generosity in sharing your music and ideas. Professor Jim McElwaine has been my mentor at Purchase College and has always been available for advice and insights regarding the material in this book. Bassist Todd Coolman is the Director of Jazz Performance at Purchase College and an excellent author. His expert help and advice were both educational and a confidence boost; thank you. Years ago I worked on a book with the man who, years before that, taught me how to sight-read, author Arnie Berle. We never completed the book project but the seed was planted for what eventually became this book, and I thank Arnie for that. I want to give props to all the cats I've studied with, recorded with, and gigged with over the years. I am also thankful for all the historic recordings by the greats of jazz. Last, I would like to thank and dedicate this book to my wife Kathleen, my sons Eugene and John, and my mother Lydia. All together you were and continue to be my source of inspiration.

Cheers!

Doug Munro

CONTENTS/CD TRACKING

Page Number **CD Track**

CHAPTER ONE:
Major Scale (Ionian Mode)

The **major scale** and its subsequent modes are made up of seven notes arranged in a specific order of whole and half steps.

The arrangement of whole and half steps in the major scale is W-W-H-W-W-W-H.

Example 1 shows a C major scale in 1st position.

Every scale you learn should be played all across the fingerboard. There are different approaches to doing this. One cool way is playing the scale in every possible position, starting on the root and playing three notes per string. By starting on the root, you will avoid the modal feel of playing the scale in different positions.

Example 2 shows the C major scale played in every position across the fingerboard using three notes per string.

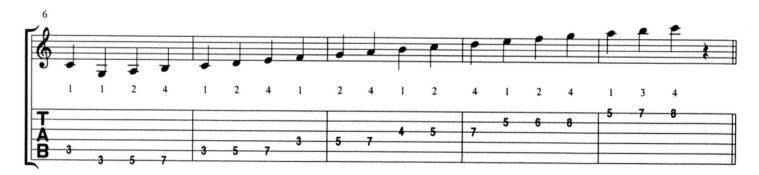

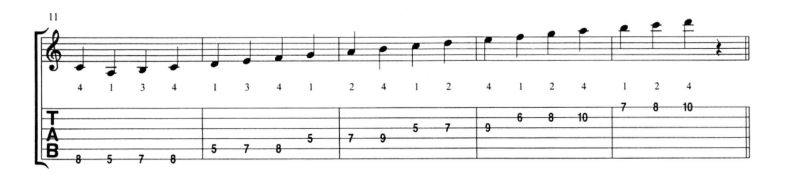

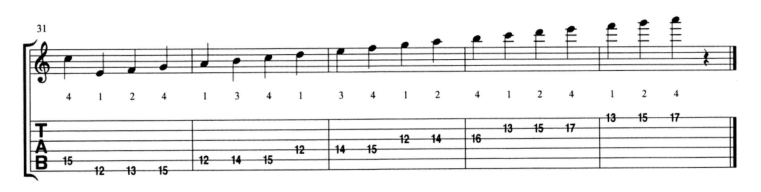

Major Scale Riffs

Example 3 is a Louis Armstrong type of riff using the major scale. There is a nice **syncopated** feel here with **phrases** that cross the bar lines. There is a chromatic approach note in bar 3 and a chromatic passing note in bar 4. Notice how most of the **accents** happen on the "and"s of beats. All of these techniques, syncopation, phrasing, and accenting weak beats help define what jazz is. Louis Armstrong was one of the key people who invented and refined this style of music. Many people tend to remember Louis Armstrong as a nice old man who sang "Hello Dolly" with a gravely voice, but he was one of the people who invented jazz. He was the first cat.

 Examples 4 and 5: Here are two **Charlie Christian**-style riffs on a major scale. Example 4 uses an odd group of notes (3) played in an even rhythm (eighth notes). This creates a nice syncopated feel. There is a flurry of **triplets** in bar 4. Notice bar 3 and 5 are the same except for the **octave**. This adds a nice **symmetry** to the phrase. Example 5 uses an **arpeggiated** type of line followed by a syncopated rhythm on the root. This riff ends with a **chromatic approach note** to the fifth and third of the C major scale, further strengthening the strong harmonic feel of the line.

CD 1B
Ex. 4

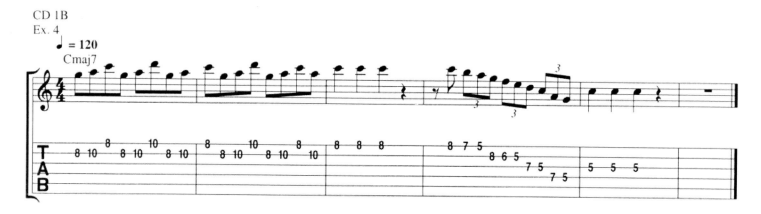

CD 1C
Ex. 5

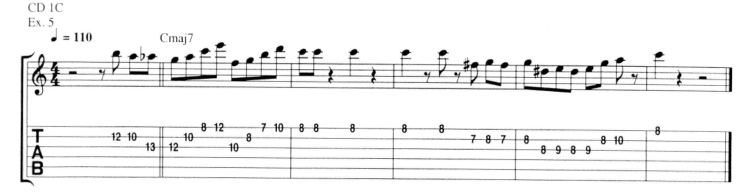

Major Chords

Chords are three or more notes played at the same time. They are traditionally built in thirds; these are known as **triads.** Later on we will build chords in fourths (quartal harmony).

Example 6 shows the **major triad** and its **inversions.** We will build our chords with the root on the 6th string, 5th string, and 4th string. As you will notice, even though our chords are built in thirds (C, E, G) they do not lay that way on the guitar. What is important here is the lowest note. There is an inversion for every note of the chord, **root position, 1st inversion** (3rd in bass), and **2nd inversion** (5th in bass).

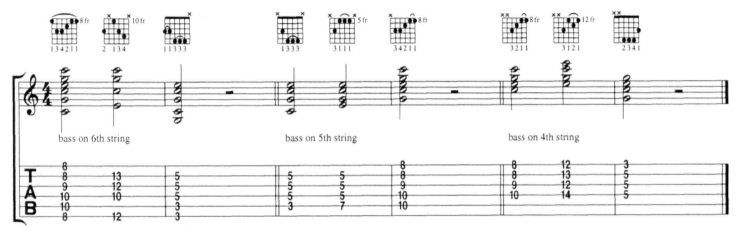

Example 7 adds another note a third above the 5th of the chord; this note is the **major 7.** With the addition of the major 7, we now have another inversion of the chord, the **3rd inversion** (7th in the bass). Again, notice that chords on the guitar do not always lay out in a 1-3-5-7 order. There are other ways to finger major and major 7 chords, and we will use many different fingerings throughout this book. I encourage you to come up with fingerings for chords that suit your fingers and your ear.

Memorize each example and make sure that you practice each example in every key!

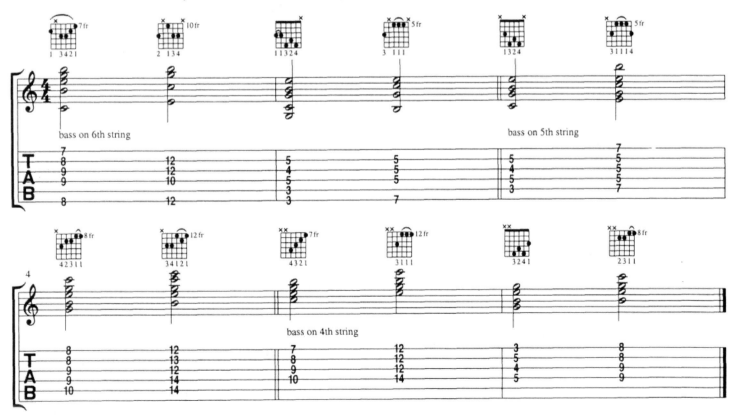

Major Chord Riffs

Example 8 is a chord riff using our Cmaj7 chord and its inversions. You can use **chord inversions** and **partial chords** in imaginative ways to make your comping exciting and supportive. This riff starts with a **chromatic approach** to the Cmaj7 chord from a half step below. In bar 2 there is a nice line created by alternating a chord inversion and the note on top of the chord. We also use the note D, which creates a **major 9** sound. There is a symmetry to this phrase and the use of accents and a **crescendo-decrescendo** to add an emotive feel. All the chords in this example are Cmaj7.

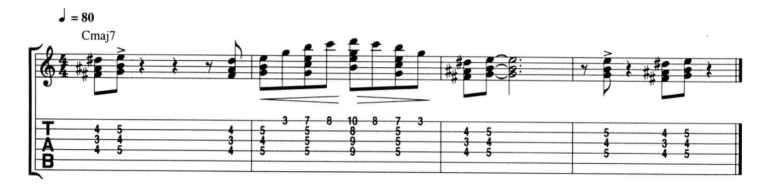

Example 9 is a little more straight-ahead four-to-the-bar comping. Notice that the chords still create their own **line**. The pay-off in this chord riff comes in the bar 4 with a nice rhythmic release and a **linear expression of the harmony.** I like to think of chords as a choir of voices each singing a line. If you can think of chords in a more linear or horizontal way as opposed to a vertical, up-and-down event, your comping will really open up. The great chord players like **Joe Pass, Barney Kessel,** and **Joe Puma** all have this approach happening.

Major 6, 9, and 6/9 Chords

Jazz harmony is all about the upper extensions of chords. If you take the note C and build up in thirds, you will get 1, 3, 5, 7, 9, 11, 13, 15, or C, E, G, B, D, F, A, C. The use of upper extensions in chords is one of the things that makes jazz sound different from other forms of popular music. The 6th (or 13th if there is a 7th present) and the 9th are often used to make major chords sound hipper. Below are some classic fingerings for guitar. I encourage you to take any of your major chord fingerings and inversions and try adding the 6th or 9th; come up with your own expression of these harmonies. I have left out the 4th or 11th (if there is a 7th present). We will look at these later when I discuss suspended chords.

Example 10 shows some common **voicings** for C major 6 (C6) chords. As you explore these, you will discover that the major 6 chord is the same as a minor 7 chord in 1st inversion (G6 is the same as Em7).

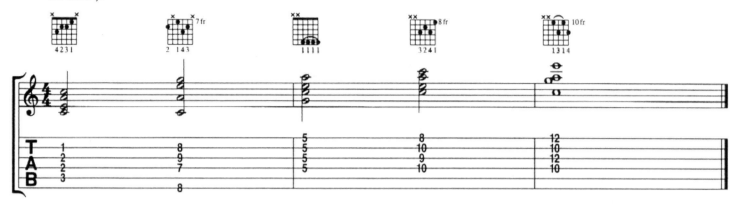

Example 11 has C major 9 (Cmaj9) voicings. Notice how I included the major 7 in all the chords. Also, check out that **the Cmaj9 chord is really a G triad (G, B, D) over C,** what we call a polychord. You can have a triad with the 9 in it, but technically it would be called a C add 9. Don't get too hung up over classical **keyboard terminology because it doesn't always fit exactly with the guitar.** If you play a major 9 chord and don't play the 3rd (E), it is technically a C Major 7 sus2. On guitar we often drop notes to grab upper extensions, and guitarists and piano players often build chords in **stacked fourths** to purposely stay away from a 1, 3, 5, etc., sound. So make the color of the chord take precedent over the theory. Theoretical constructs came from an analysis of music. **Remember: The music came first.**

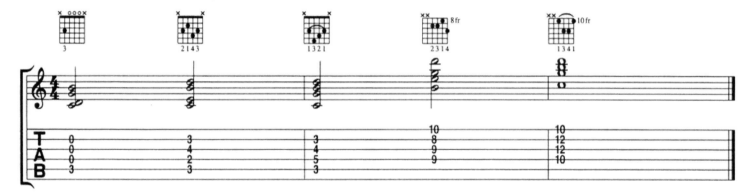

Major 6, 9 and 6/9 Chord Riffs

Example 12 shows that C 6/9 chords have a lot of these **stacked fourths voicings.** Building chords in fourths instead of thirds is called **quartal harmony.** Notice that the chords in bar 2/beat 3, bar 3/beat 3, and bar 4 all have the same fingering shape. You just move them to different frets on the neck. The great jazz piano player **McCoy Tyner** is a good person to check out to hear these voicings. Many guitar players such as **Wes Montgomery** and **George Benson** used the 6/9 chords. They have become a readily identifiable sound on jazz guitar.

♩ = 120

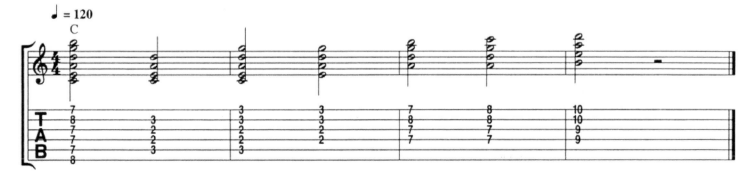

Example 13 uses some of the **C6, maj9, and 6/9 voicings combined.** There is a **rhythmic and melodic sequence** (in the top voice) throughout this riff. There are slight variations in the note duration. This usually occurs naturally but I wanted to emphasize the idea in this example. You will also note that these **chords are all voiced on the first four strings.** This is a nice range for comping with other instruments. It allows your voicings to sit on top of the harmony and avoid potential clashes in the lower register. It will take a minute to master some of these exercises, but it is worth it. You will soon have under your fingers and in your ear the type of phrasing and fingerings used by the great traditional chord compers from **Freddie Green** to **Wes Montgomery.**

Suspended 4 and Suspended 2 Chords

When you see a chord symbol that has the abbreviated word "sus" in it, it means the 3rd of that chord is not there. It is replaced by either the fourth or second note of that chord's related scale. **The chord loses its major or minor quality because there is no 3rd.** Theoretically, a suspended chord is followed by a resolution: the sus4 note moves down to the 3rd or the sus2 note moves up to the 3rd. However, in jazz, sus4 and sus2 chords do not always resolve.

Examples 14 and 15 show some fingerings for suspended chords. Some will be more awkward than others depending on the size of your hand. **Try to find ways of playing that work for you.** Don't try to conform to some preconceived notion you may have of "proper technique." The audience can only hear what you play; the average listener will have no idea about how you are executing what you are playing on your instrument.

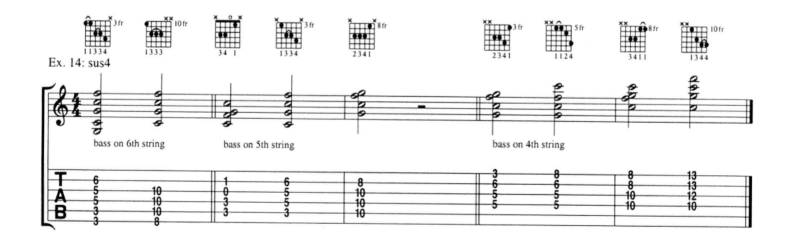

Ex. 14: sus4

bass on 6th string   bass on 5th string   bass on 4th string

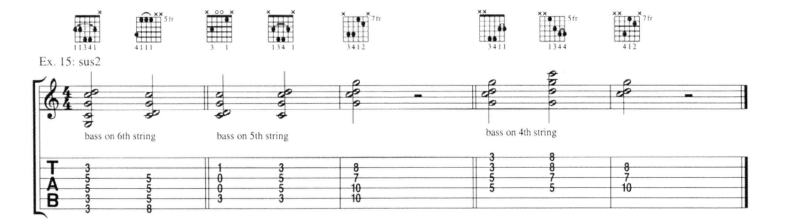

Ex. 15: sus2

bass on 6th string   bass on 5th string   bass on 4th string

Suspended 4 and Suspended 2 Chord Riffs

Example 16 uses long notes to exaggerate the airy feeling of the sus4 and sus2 chords. Using the sus chords in this way, you can hear how we've moved from **Louis Armstrong** and **Django Reinhardt** to **Miles Davis** and **John Coltrane.** We have temporarily time warped.

CD 4A

♩ = 100

Example 17 also has a floating feeling but with more rhythmic urgency. **Tempo, dynamics, and rhythmic density** are great tools for creating a particular mood whether it's happy, sad, angry, and so on.

CD 4B

♩ = 120

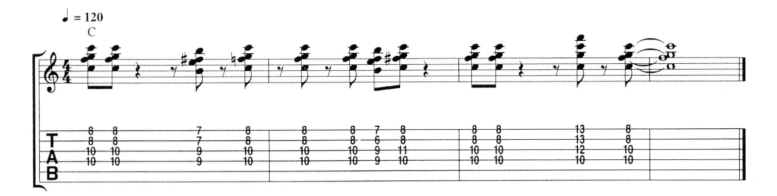

Major Arpeggios

An arpeggio is a chord played one at a time. For example, the C major arpeggio is C, E, G. Arpeggio-style playing is one of the cornerstones of jazz improvisation. It is a method of really spelling the harmony you are on or spelling some other harmony you want to superimpose. Arpeggios also help the guitar player start playing along the fingerboard through different positions as opposed to the up-and-down, sticking-in-one-position, wearing-your-frets-out-in-one-spot approach.

Example 18 is a systematic presentation of a **one-octave C major arpeggio** in many practical fingerings. Try all the fingerings and then find the ones that work best for you. Because of the number of frets on different guitars, I have omitted the fingerings that repeat above the 12th fret; just use the fingerings that correspond below the 12th fret. You should play this exercise across your entire fingerboard. **Try playing this and all of the exercises in all keys.** A good way to do this is by using the **cycle of descending 5ths** (C, F, B♭, E♭, A♭, D♭, G♭, B, E, A, D, G). Don't forget to use your metronome!

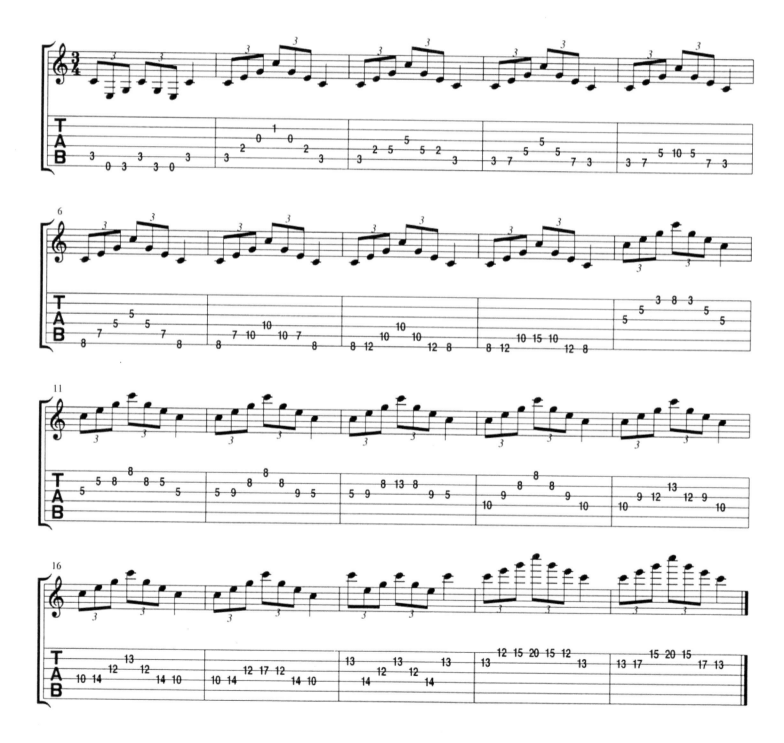

Major Arpeggio Riffs

CD
5A
Example 19 is in the style of **Charlie Christian** and the legendary gypsy swing guitarist **Django Reinhardt.** These are all chord tones played in a **sequential pattern** descending and its mirror opposite ascending. The riff starts with a classic triplet blast-off. Notice the accents are all on the up-beats.

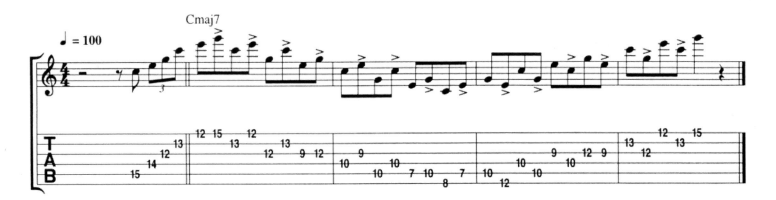

CD
5B
Example 20 uses the concept of the **lower chromatic approach note** to each chord tone. You will notice the major seventh is really being used as a chromatic approach to the basic triadic chord tones. The use of **double stops** (two notes played at the same time) in this riff is very common to this traditional jazz sound. This example may seem a little challenging, but hang in there and work it out.

Major 7 and Major 6 Arpeggios

Example 21: Here again is a systematic presentation of a **one-octave C major arpeggio.** The difference here is that I've added the major 7 (B) to our pre-existing triad (C, E, G). We now have a four-note chord instead of the previous three-note chord.

> **Assignment:** You should be getting the hang of this arpeggio thing by now. **On your own, write out the fingerings for the major 6 arpeggio (C, E, G, A).**

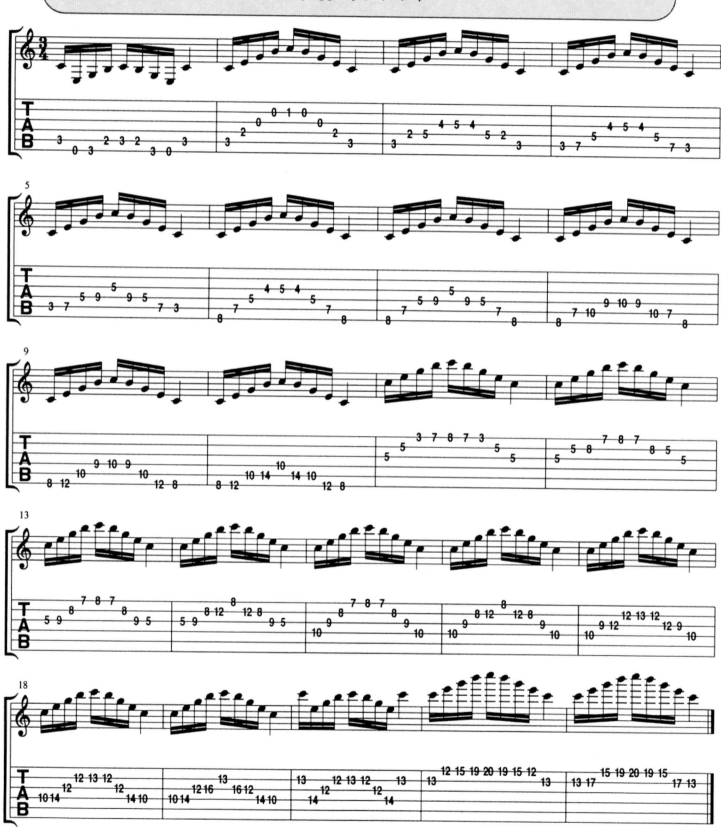

Major 7 and Major 6 Arpeggio Riffs

CD 6A **Example 22** has a repeated short **motif** that is extended into a large descending line in the bar 3. Notice there is a **sequential pattern** to the descending riff.

CD 6B **Example 23** starts out with a wide interval spacing between the notes. They are in groups of two but are played with a triplet rhythm. This creates a **polyrhythmic** feel of two against three. The rest of the riff consists of groups of three notes played in eighth notes. The odd grouping of note sequences and rhythm values is standard jazz practice. **Wes Montgomery** and **Jim Hall** are two of many to really jump on this approach.

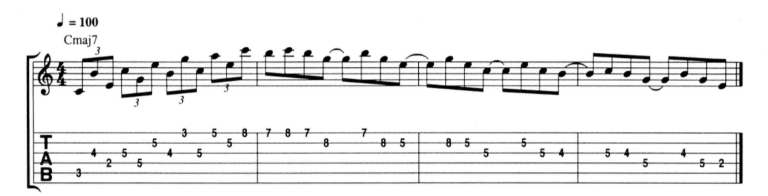

CD 6C **Example 24** is a study in **note density contrasts.** The riff starts in an odd place (the "and" of beat 1) and proceeds to go through triplets to sixteenths that cross the bar line going back to eighths and ending in a sustained **trill.** (The trill is between the notes B and C.)

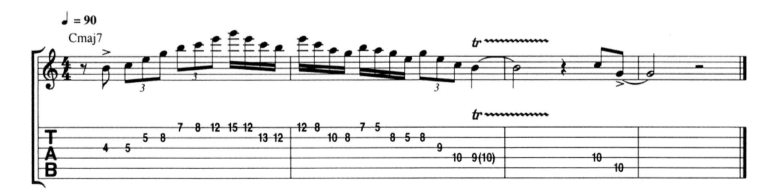

Diatonic Major Scale Tone Chords

It's now time to take the major scale, chords, and arpeggios and various riffs that we've looked at and put them to use in an actual song format. There are many approaches you can take when improvising. One approach is to **solo in the "key" of the song,** or section of the song, you are in. How do you know what chords are diatonic to a certain key? The answer is learning your **diatonic scale tone chords.**

Example 25: Here is an example of the scale tone chords in the key of C. What I have done is written a **C major scale** and then built up a **four-note chord, in 3rds, above each note.** You will see that results in a series of major 7, minor 7, dominant 7, and minor 7(♭5) chords. Notice that these chords are written in sequence (1, 3, 5, 7). **These are not guitar voicings.**

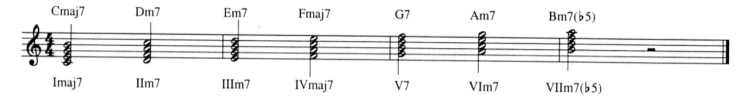

This order of chord types will be the same in every key. We use Roman numerals to identify the chords: this way we can play a specific chord progression in any key (for example, IIm7-V7-Imaj7).

> **In any key, the diatonic major scale tone chords are as follows:**
> Imaj7 IIm7 IIIm7 IVmaj7 V7 VIm7 VIIm7(♭5)
>
> What would a IIm7-V7-Imaj7 in the key of C be? _____
>
> What would it be in the key of F? _____
>
> What about a Imaj7-VIm7-IIm7-V7 in B♭? _____
>
> Practice figuring these out.

It is critical to know all of your major scales and key signatures. All Western European harmony is based on it. If you really understand and can hear your scales and key signatures, you will have the necessary foundation for the harmonic discussions that follow in this book.

We have not worked on all the chords shown on this page yet; that's okay. What is important to understand here is that all chords that are diatonic to a major key contain only notes that are found in the major scale of that key. Therefore, you can play one major scale over all the diatonic chords.

The best way to understand this is to see and hear the concept in action. In the following example, I am going to take everything we have done (scales, chords, arpeggios) and use them in a diatonic chord progression.

Summary Solo #1

CD 7

Example 26 is in the style of **Django Reinhardt** with a little **Charlie Christian** and **Satchmo** thrown in. All the chords used are diatonic to the key of C major. The song is a standard 32-bar (measure) A-A-B-A form, and each section is eight bars long.

Note:

1) The solo doesn't focus on each chord change as much as it uses patterns from the C major scale.
2) The solo is **thematic**, using a **central riff (bar 1).** Thematic ideas can come from many sources, including the melody of the song, a melody from another song, or a riff idea.
3) I used a lot of **sequential playing** here to get my ideas across. This tends to make solos sound compositional, focused, and deliberate.
4) The entire second A section is a series of **descending 6ths.** Different sections use **rhythmic variation, double stops, and chordal patterns.**

This solo and other examples are presented at a medium tempo. Playing slowly with perfect technique and clear understanding is the first step in learning to burn.

Solo #1

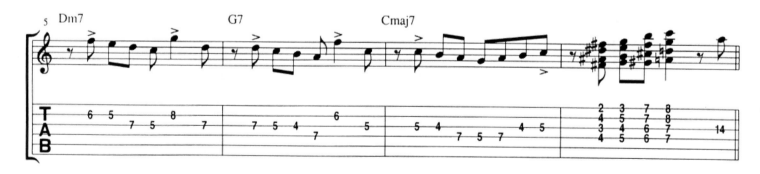

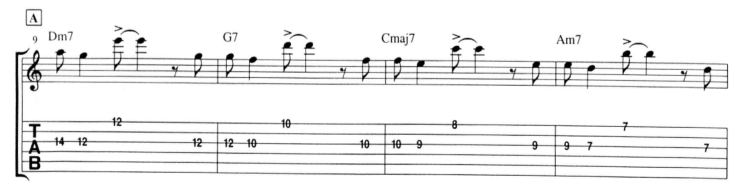

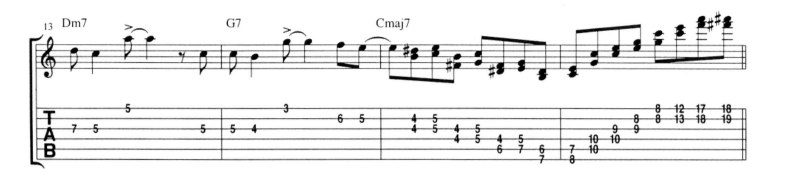

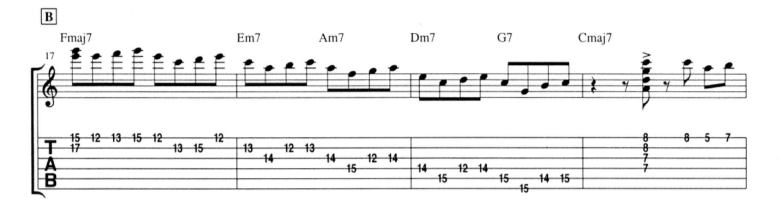

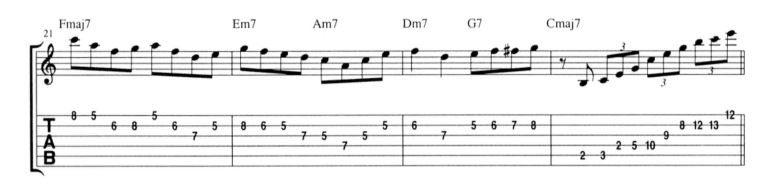

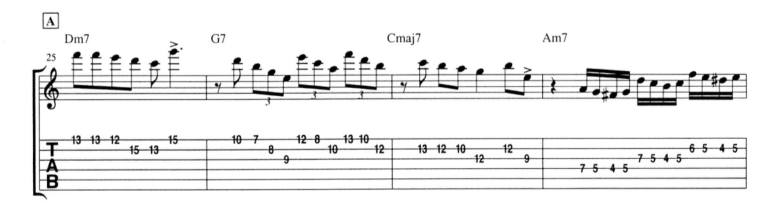

Summary Solo #2

CD 8 **Example 27** uses a slightly harder solo concept, **playing on each chord change.** You will have noticed by now that we have been **swinging the eighth notes** in our examples. The closest approximation would be to say that two eighth notes are played like the first and third notes of a triplet figure. The inspiration for this solo is a melodic bite from **Toots Thielman's "Bluesette."** The chord progression is a slightly uncommon turnaround that uses all major 7 chords. I made each chord two bars in length to make it a little easier to blow on. You will notice here that some of the phrases seem to be a little square rhythmically, starting on beat 1. In 3/4 time, it is rather common to do this because the **meter lends an odd grouping to the phrases.**

Note:

1) In bar 8, I anticipated the next chord change (Cmaj7) by playing an arpeggio with many of the notes in the upcoming chord. This sounded okay on the chord I was on (D♭maj7) because that chord is functioning as a sub for the V7 chord (G7). Don't worry—we'll deal more with that later on.

2) Starting in bar 19, there is a **sequence of chords across the changes.** The continuous dotted quarter notes create a temporary "two against three" feel. **Wes Montgomery** often did this and other interesting rhythmic chordal playing in his solos. This is often originated from the imitation of piano players or big band horn sections.

3) The entire solo is full of **motivic and sequential ideas.** The lines that connect each chord change are usually either a half or one whole step apart. This leads to seamless connections between chords and the smooth continuation of your line. A lot of the phrases extend over the changing of the chords.

Solo #2

CHAPTER TWO:
Dorian Mode

The **Dorian mode** is a scale made up of seven notes arranged in a specific order of whole and half steps. This order originally came from the natural notes from D to D. This was the second of the seven Greek modes. **The Dorian mode is the same as a major scale, beginning and ending on the second note. For instance, D Dorian is a C major scale played from D to D.** This mode sounds minor because of the lowered third note. Jazz players have embraced the Dorian mode for playing on minor chords because of its natural sixth degree.

The arrangement of whole and half steps in the Dorian mode is W-H-W-W-W-H-W.

Example 28 shows an F Dorian mode in 1st position.

All modes are scales but not all scales are modes. I have picked F Dorian for our examples in this chapter to get away from the key of C and its relative modes. You should **practice all that you learn in this book in every key.**

Example 29 shows the F Dorian mode played in every possible position across the fingerboard using three notes per string. Notice in every position that I start with the root (F). This is to reinforce the Dorian sound.

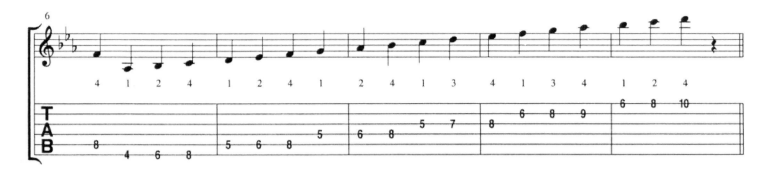

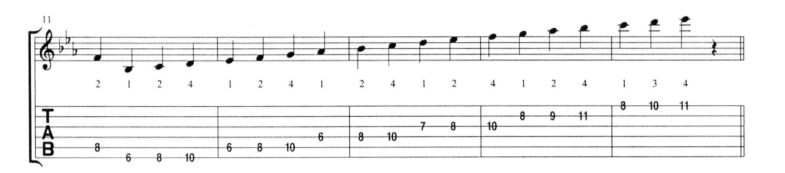

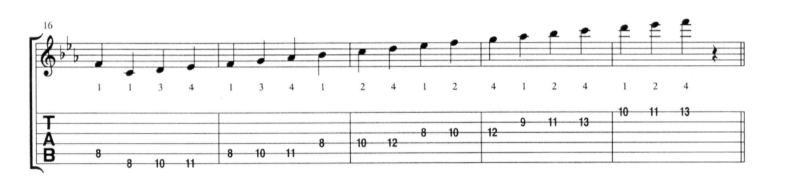

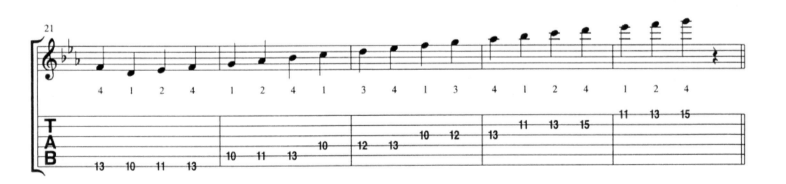

Dorian Mode Riffs

Example 30 is a **Wes Montgomery**-style riff over an Fm7 chord. These are the famous octaves for which Wes is mostly remembered. Notice the tight rhythmic motif that drives this riff. To really make this sound authentic, put your pick down and play this riff with your thumb. You have to mute the strings you are not playing with your left hand and the heel of your right hand. It takes a minute to get this technique happening, but it's definitely worth the trouble. The thumb gives the notes a warmer tone.

Example 31 emphasizes the **9th** (G) in a repeating figure. This is another trademark of Wes and many of his contemporaries. Making use of the **upper extensions** of the chords is the bread and butter of jazz sounds. The second half of this riff is a descending sequence of four-note groupings that start on the weak beats and cross the bar lines. These are just a series of eighth notes, but the feeling is **syncopated** because of the groupings.

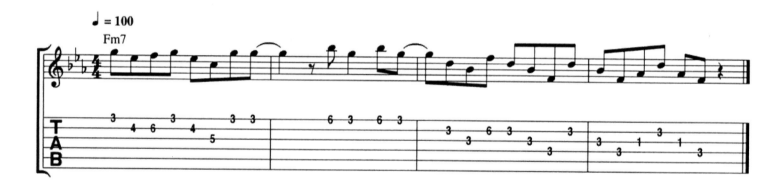

Example 32 emphasizes the **6th** (D). There is an arpeggio type of move to the 6th that is repeated. The riff ends with a cascade of triplets using the extension notes, the 9th and the 6th.

Minor and Minor 7 Chords

Example 33 shows the basic minor triad in some common fingerings with the root on the 6th, 5th, and 4th strings. Notice again how the chords don't usually lay out 1, ♭3, 5 on the guitar.

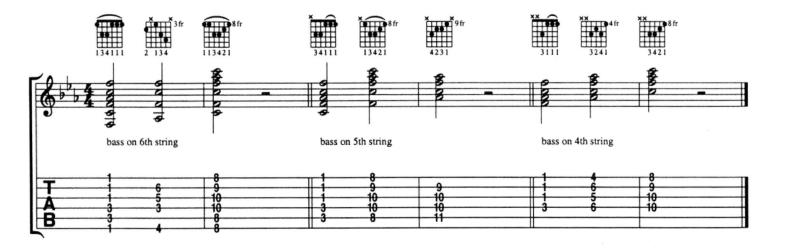

Example 34 is the minor 7 chord (1, 3, 5, ♭7) and its inversions. Notice that every minor 7 chord shown here in 1st inversion (3rd in the bass) is also a major 6 chord. For example, an Fm7 chord in 1st inversion is the same as an A♭ major 6 chord. In strict theory, there is no such thing as a major 6 chord; it is really a minor 7 chord in 1st inversion. If this seems a bit confusing, don't worry—just think of 6th chords as a cool harmonic anomaly.

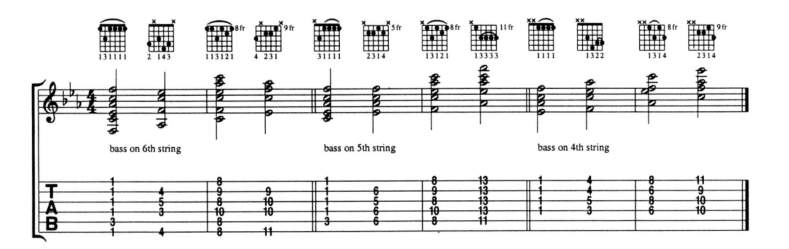

Minor Chord Riffs

Example 35 starts right on the **down-beat.** In comping, it is important to let the soloist feel secure about where the time is and where the form is. The easiest way to do this is to play a chord on the down-beat at the top of a section. This may seem a little square, but in the context of support it is not. Remember that **syncopation and odd phrasings have to be in contrast to something**—that something is the "1," the down-beat. This riff covers a lot of ground from the 1st to the 16th fret. It's good to get this linear feel into your comping. Starting in bar 2, all the **accents start hitting on the up-beats.** The major syncopation in this riff occurs in the last bar on the "and" of beat 3.

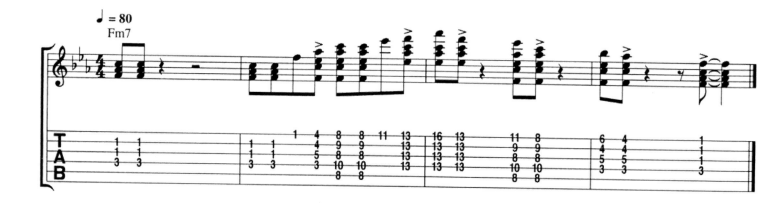

Example 36 is a chord riff that has the potential to step on the bass player's line. It's hoped that he will hear what you are comping and join in your line. This is a **basic four-to-the-floor comping feel.** You will notice I have stuck a Gm7 chord on beat 2 of the first three bars. Remember our **scale tone chords**? Well, Gm7 is the second chord in the scale tone chords of F Dorian. If you don't understand this, don't sweat it. Think of the Gm7 as a "passing chord" getting us from Fm7 in root position (beat 1) to Fm7 in 1st inversion (beat 3). The low note E is used as a **chromatic approach tone** to the beginning of each bar. I'm calling E a chromatic note because it's not part of the Fm7 chords we are using nor the F Dorian mode. Again, the major syncopation in this riff occurs in the last bar, but this time it kicks on the "and" of beat 2.

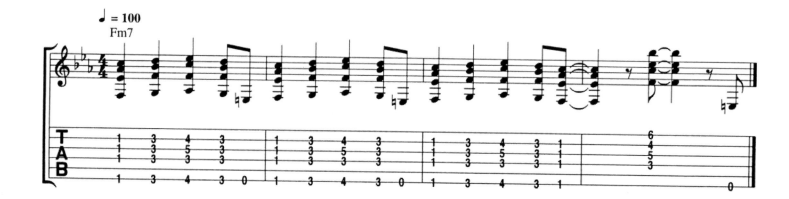

Minor 6, Minor 9, and Minor 11 Chords

Following are some common fingerings for these minor chords with upper extensions.

Example 37 is the minor 6 chord. Later you will notice that some of these fingerings look and sound like dominant 9 chords in 1st inversion or m7(♭5) chords. As we build upper extensions on chords, we start creating polychords (two different chords being sounded at the same time).

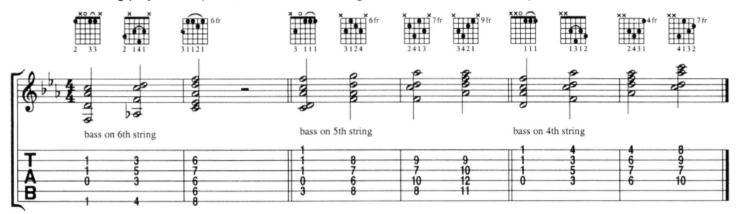

Example 38 is minor 9 chords. I did not include a lot of different fingerings here because **the 1st inversion of this chord on guitar looks like its relative major 7 chord.** For example, the Fm9 on the 6th string in 1st inversion fingers just like an A♭maj7 chord. This is another example of how you will see other basic chords in the upper extensions of a given chord. (You can see an A♭maj7 chord in an Fm9 chord: **F, A♭, C, E♭, G.**)

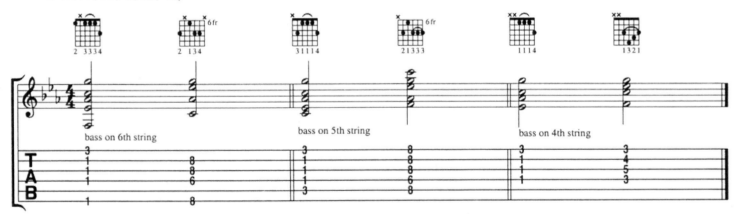

Example 39: On the minor 11 chords, you can see major 6/9 chord shapes, especially starting on the 3rd of the chord. **I substitute minor 11 chords for minor 7 chords quite often.** They sound great on guitar, giving a more floating tension to the chord. All the fingerings here are not definitive. **Please explore your own fingerings.**

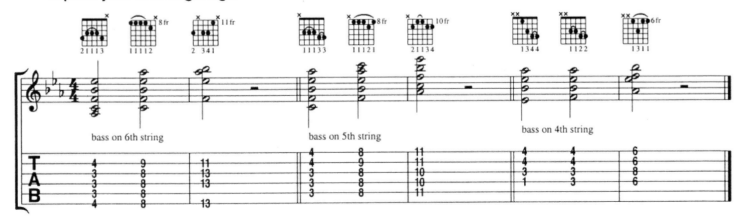

Minor 6, Minor 9, and Minor 11 Chord Riffs

In the following examples, you will see combinations of minor 6, 9, and 11 chords with some chromatic goodies thrown in. When comping, try to move away from the vertical grab-every-note-you-can approach to a more linear, melodic style. An accomplished accompanist improvises his support statement as freely as the soloist he is playing behind.

 Example 40 is a bluesy riff using a **minor 11 chord** and moving it up one whole step (diatonic move) and then up another half step (chromatic move). This creates that blues bent-note feel; this move is out of the **George Benson** book. I contrast this line with a **minor 6 chord** in a lower voicing. It gives the effect of a call and response. **Wes Montgomery** often did this in his comping and solos.

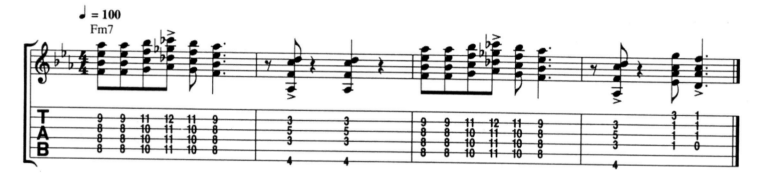

 Example 41 is a **Latin-feel** type of chord riff. You could use this on a bossa nova or any medium-feel Latin straight-eighth tune. Notice in bar 1 that I have an F minor chord with an E natural in the bass. This is commonly called a **minor(maj7) chord**. The E natural gives a tense chromatic feel to this riff, which is in the guitar style of **Joe Beck**. There is a nice open-voiced 11 chord at the end of the phrase that propels the riff into the next bar.

 Example 42 takes a different approach to chord comping. Here I have an interval stack of a perfect 4th and a whole step and found places where they work over the existing harmony (Fm7). Notice that all the notes are diatonic and yet there is a very unconventional sound. **Sequencing note clusters** in this way is a more modern approach used often by piano players such as **McCoy Tyner.**

Minor Arpeggios

We will start again here with the basic three-note minor arpeggio: 1, ♭3, 5 (Fm: F, A♭, C).

Example 43 is a one-octave **F minor arpeggio** in different fingerings on the guitar neck. At the 12th fret, the fingerings will repeat themselves sounding an octave higher. I will let you work them through. In general, as this book progresses I will count on you to complete some of these harmonic tasks yourself.

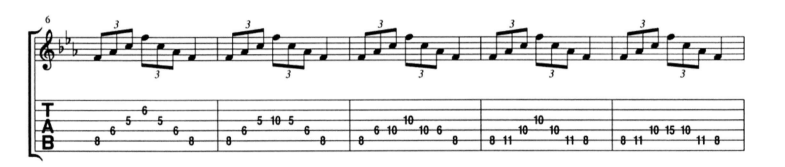

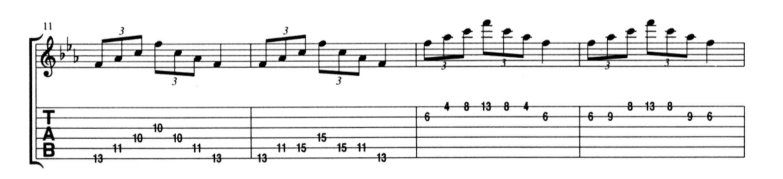

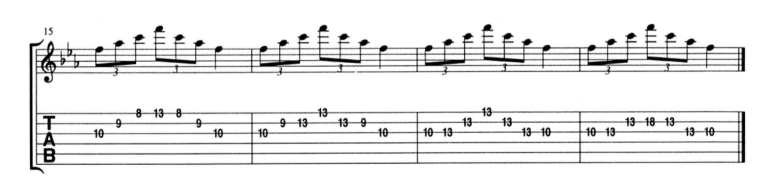

Minor Arpeggio Riffs

CD 12A **Example 44** is a bluesy sounding riff out of the **Wes Montgomery** book. Wes had a great blues feel to everything he played. A lot of famous jazz players have said, "If you can't play blues, you can't play jazz." This riff is a repeated statement with the payoff coming in bar 4 with the triplet line. There is a rhythmic push on the "and of 4" in bar 1 to help the line swing.

CD 12B **Example 45** starts with a phrase reminiscent of the song "Move." It has a nice rhythmic call and response.

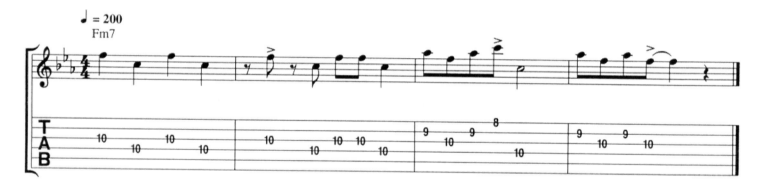

CD 12C **Example 46** is a straight-up minor arpeggio starting on the 5th (C). This riff's strength is that it covers a lot of ground (2 1/2 octaves). This is in the **Django Reinhardt** style and is very European (classical) sounding.

Minor 7, Minor 6, and Minor 9 Arpeggios

Example 47 highlights a variety of fingerings for an Fm7 one-octave arpeggio. After practicing these a while, you should start combining the one-octave arpeggios to build two- and three-octave arpeggios that traverse the fingerboard.

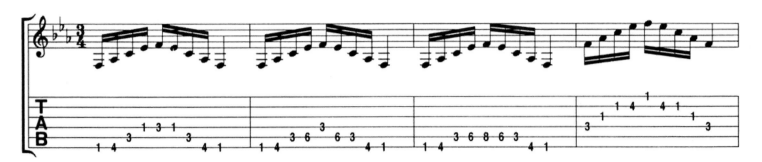

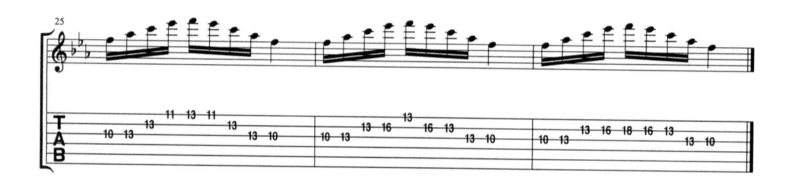

I have not repeated the fingerings above the 12th fret again. You can do that yourself. I want you to go and do the minor 6 (F, A♭, C, D) and minor 9 (F, A♭, C, E♭, G) arpeggios as well.

Check this out: If you keep building a chord or arpeggio in thirds, you will get these notes: 1 (F), ♭3 (A♭), 5 (C), 7 (E♭), 9 (G), 11 (B♭), 13 (D, also the 6th), 15 (F).

You wind up with all the notes in the F Dorian mode. I look at the notes in a scale as functions of a chord or arpeggio. For example, this is how I think of the notes in the F Dorian mode: F (root), G (9th), A♭ (♭3), B♭ (11th), C (5), D (6th or 13th), E♭ (7th).

Thinking of scales in this way allows you to bring a stronger sense of harmony to your linear excursions.

Minor 7, Minor 6, and Minor 9 Arpeggio Riffs

CD

13A
Example 48 is an arpeggio riff that uses the **6th and the 9th.** The riff is repetitive and builds in length. Check out the **chromatic approach tone** (B) in bar 4.

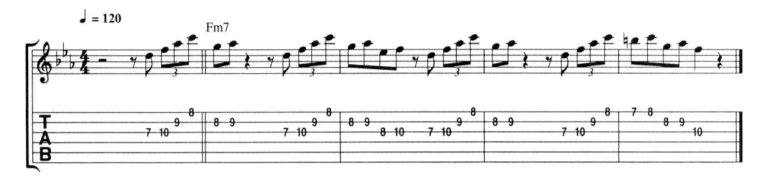

CD

13B
Example 49 has two interesting things happening. First, the harmony is concealed in bar 1 and 3. I don't play the root or the 3rd of the chord (Fm7). The second interesting aspect of this riff is the **phrasing across the bar line.** It almost appears as if the riff is in 4/4 time.

CD

13C
Example 50 is a **Pat Martino**-style riff. Pat is the master of minor. Check out the use of the **major 7 (E natural)** to launch the lines in bars 1 and the end of 2. Notice how **the line is staggered.** It starts on the "and" of 1 in bar 1 and resumes on the "and" of 4 in bar 2.

Summary Solo #3

CD
14

Example 51 is a **32-bar A-B-A-B form.** The song is in a medium tempo in 3/4 time. Notice that **all the chords are diatonic to the key of F Dorian (E♭ major).** This allows us to play the F Dorian mode over all the changes. There are many other solo options here, but soloing in the key (F Dorian) is what is demonstrated here.

Note:

1) In bar 9, there is an A♭6 instead of an A♭maj7. I did this because the **A♭6 is an Fm7 in 1st inversion** (remember?) and I wanted that sound.
2) The solo starts out on the note G, which is the 9th of an Fm7 chord. This move is straight out of the **Wes Montgomery** book.
3) I purposely avoid the 3rd (A♭) of the F Dorian mode, which doesn't come in until bar 5.
4) In bar 18, there is a **Pat Martino** type of riff using the major 7 note (E), which moves right into another Wes-style riff.
5) In bar 26, there is one last flurry of 16th notes. This is a sequential riff that is repeated a perfect 5th down. This line is typical of sax players.

Solo #3

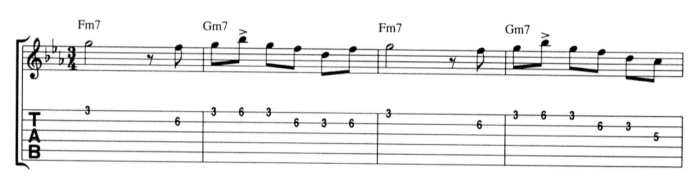

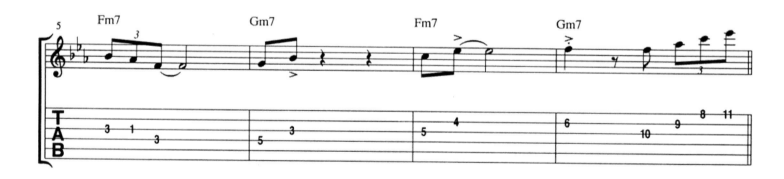

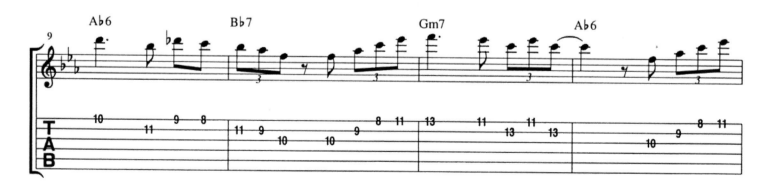

Summary Solo #4

 Example 52 is an up-tempo blues in cut time. So although it feels like a 12-bar blues, it is actually written as a **24-bar blues** in 4/4 time. All the chords here are diatonic to the key of F Dorian (E♭ major). Even though this is a swing-style piece, you will notice that **the eighth notes are played straight.** At up-tempos, eighth notes straighten out and are played as sixteenth notes are at slower tempos. Try swinging your eights at fast tempos and you will immediately hear why they are played straight (they sound weird swung).

Note:

1) The first line in this piece emphasizes the **raised 6th (D).** This line then **chromatically descends until it hits a diatonic note (C)** and then ends in a little blues type of turn.

2) The main **rhythmic theme** that ties this chorus together can be found in bars 7, 15, and 23. Notice they happen at the end of each harmonic section.

3) The second large phrase starts at the pickup to bar 9. This phrase is an arpeggio line that is diatonic to F Dorian but appears to sound out a couple of chords (Fm7, Gm7) over the harmony (B♭7), which creates a nice **polychord** feel. This line also ends in the rhythmic figure using an Fm9 chord.

4) The last line that begins in bar 17 is just a straight-up F Dorian mode that starts on beat 3. It's played descending using eighth notes, but the notes descend in groups of three, again giving a **"three against two" feel.** This line also ends in our little rhythm, but this final time it's just the note F.

Solo #4

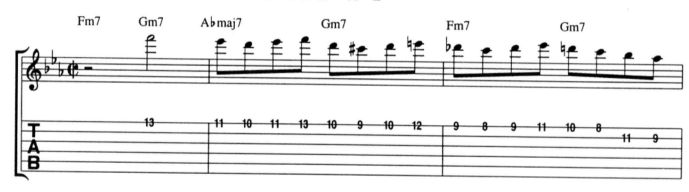

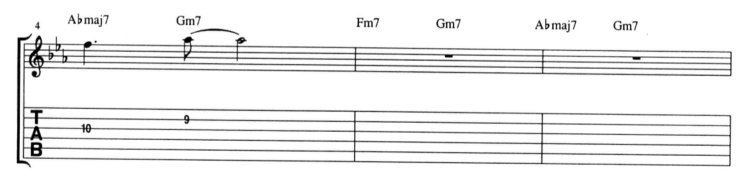

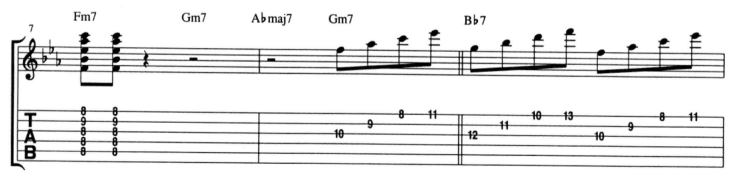

CHAPTER THREE:
Mixolydian Mode (Dominant 7 Scale)

The **Mixolydian mode** is a scale made up of seven notes arranged in a specific order of whole and half steps. This order originally came from the natural notes from G to G. So the Mixolydian mode is the same as a major scale played from the 5th note. Hence, this was the fifth of the seven Greek modes. This mode is like a major scale except that the 7th note is lowered a half step. This is the scale and chord (dominant 7) that has the most possible alterations attached to it. It is a tension chord.

The arrangement of whole and half steps in the Mixolydian mode is W-W-H-W-W-H-W.

Example 53 shows a C Mixolydian mode in 1st position.

All modes are scales but not all scales are modes. I have picked C Mixolydian for our examples. We have looked at the key of C major, F Dorian (E♭ major), and now C Mixolydian (F major). You should **practice all that you learn in this book in every key.**

Example 54 shows the C Mixolydian mode played in every possible position across the fingerboard using three notes per string. Notice that in every position I start with the root (C). This is to reinforce the Mixolydian, or dominant 7, sound.

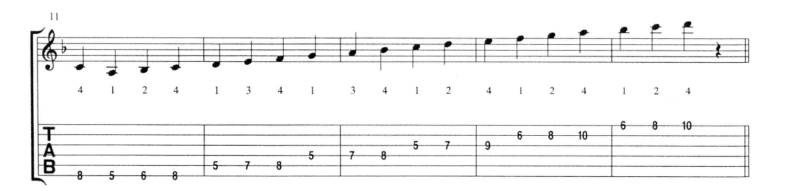

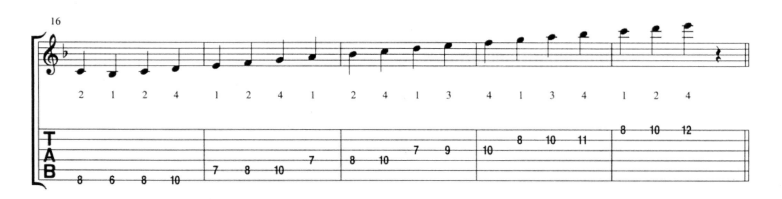

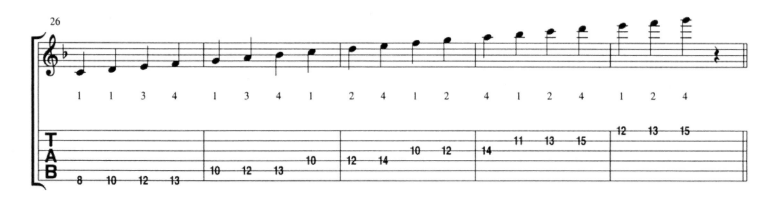

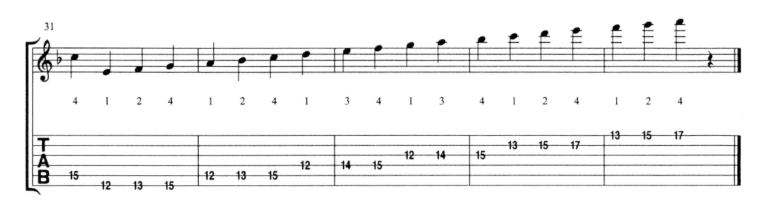

Mixolydian Mode Riffs

Example 55 is a riff in the style of **Eddie Lang.** It has a strong blues feel to it with a rather classical type of run that ends with the same blues turn. This combination of Eastern European and American blues influences was common to Eddie Lang and many of the jazz pioneers.

Example 56 is another **Wes Montgomery**-style octave riff in 3/4. Notice the repeated triplet figure that ends in a bluesy statement using the ♯9 (D♯). Don't forget to put down the pick and play this with your thumb.

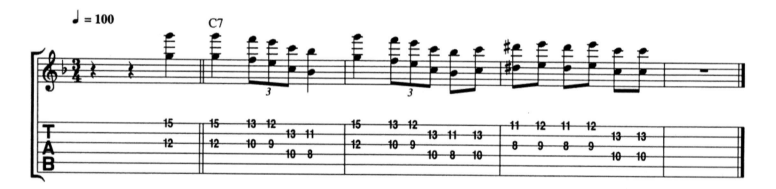

Example 57 is in the style of **Grant Green.** The line uses the ♭7 (B♭) as a pivot note in bars 1 and 2. The line climaxes in a wicked descending triplet figure.

Dominant 7 Chords

Example 58 is the C dominant 7 chord written in root, 1st, 2nd, and 3rd positions on the 6th, 5th, and 4th strings. There are many other fingerings, and I encourage you to explore and **use fingerings that sound and feel good for your expression.**

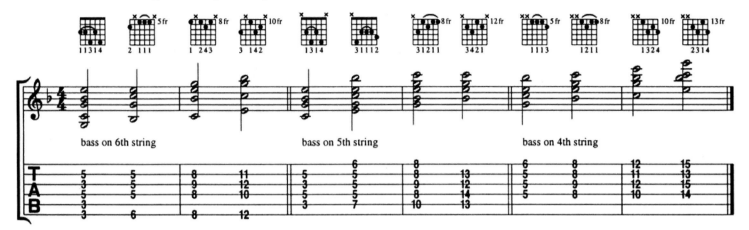

Dominant 9 Chords

Example 59 shows some of the common fingerings for C dominant 9th chords.

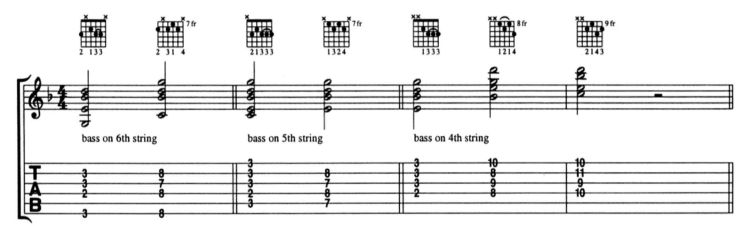

Dominant 13 Chords

Example 60 shows some typical C dominant 13th fingerings. Notice that as we add more extensions (7th, 9th, 13th), we drop more and more of the fundamental chord tones.

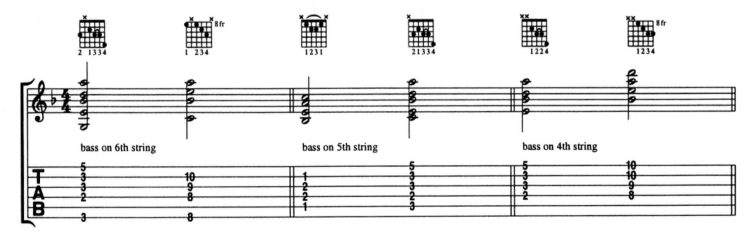

Dominant 7, 9, 13 Chord Riffs

CD 17A **Example 61** is a riff in 3/4 that is similar to the opening riff of the song "All Blues" by Miles Davis. The first chord is a small C7 with a crushed tone, **D♯ (the sharp 9).** The second chord creates a **polychord, F/C.** The third chord also implies another triad, **E♭m/C.**

CD 17B **Example 62** is a swing-style eighth-note riff that ascends and then does a big glissando down to the final two chords that use the ♯9 and ♯5 as chromatic passing notes.

CD 17C **Example 63** is interesting in that a lot of the upper extensions are not harmonized but are played as single notes. The first beat in bar 1 is technically not a chord because it is only two notes, B♭ and E (the ♭7 and 3rd of C7). Remember that in context, your ear will hear the C dominant sound, and if you are playing with a bass player, he will spell out the harmony anyway. The last thing to check out is that I used the same notes to start and end with, but they are in different positions on the neck. I did this to make the last bar easier to play.

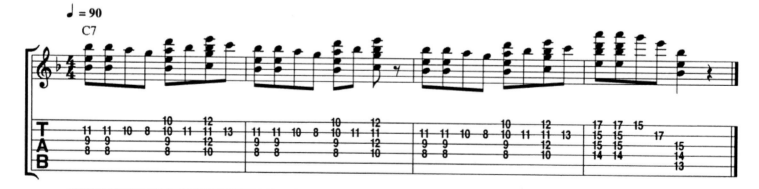

As an exercise, go back and put C dominant 7 fingerings under the single notes in Example 63.

Dominant 7 Arpeggios

We are going to start with the four-note dominant 7 arpeggio (1, 3, 5, ♭7). Using a C7 chord as our example, the notes will be C, E, G, B♭.

Example 64 is a collection of one-octave dominant 7 arpeggios. I did not repeat the forms above the 12th fret: you can do that. Practice these arpeggios all over the neck in every key—really. Connect them to form two- and three-octave arpeggios. Find fingerings that work for you.

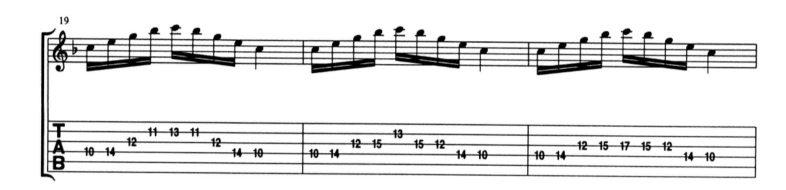

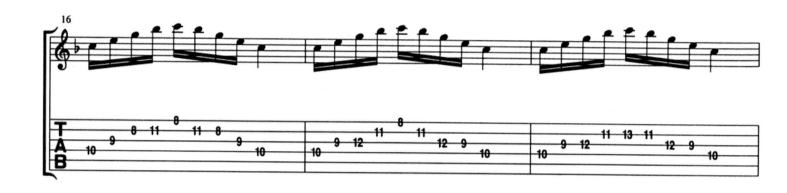

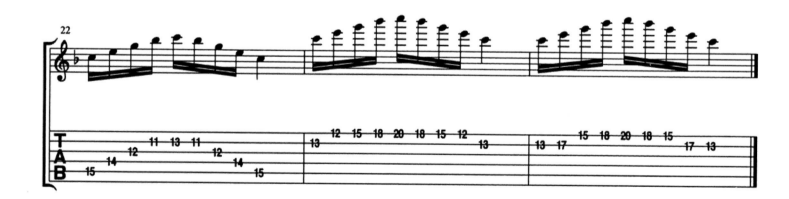

Once again, I would like you to go back and insert the 9 and 13 into these arpeggios. You will notice that if you insert enough extensions, you will wind up playing the dominant 7 scale, calling each scale tone a chord tone (root, 9th, 3rd, 11th, 5th, 13th, ♭7th).

Dominant 7 Arpeggio Riffs

CD
18A **Example 65** is a 2 1/2-octave arpeggio that starts on beat 2. The descending section in bar 2 is in groups of three, but each group of three starts on the last beat of each triplet. This gives a nice rhythmic push to the line. Notice the chromatic passing tone (B) in bar 2.

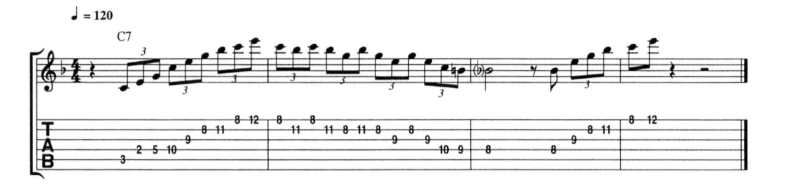

CD
18B **Example 66** is an early **George Benson**-style riff using **arpeggio fragments** in three different octaves. Notice the use of the **#9 (D#).** This gives the line a bluesy feel.

CD
18C **Example 67** is a line that uses **two different classic rhythms.** I have heard everybody using these; I don't know who can lay claim to them.

Dominant 9 and 13 Arpeggio Riffs

CD **19A** **Example 68** has a **repeating rhythmic riff** in the style of **George Benson**. The line is a tight combination of eighth notes, triplets, and sixteenth notes. This riff has a call-and-response feel.

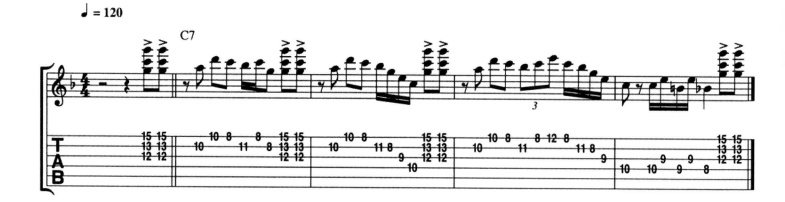

CD **19B** **Example 69** is an up-tempo riff that pedals off the root (C). It ends in a cascade of two partial C dominant arpeggios. This line is more horn-like in origin.

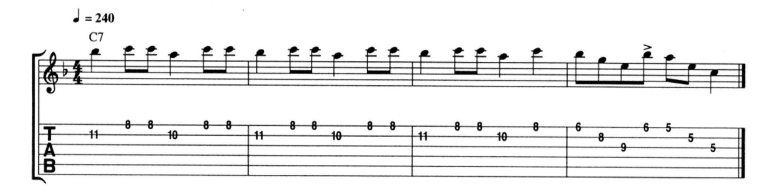

CD **19C** **Example 70** makes use of the **9th (D)** and the **13th (A)**. The line starts in a lower register and moves to a higher register to finish. In classical lingo, this would be called an **antecedent and consequent** phrase, or as we would call it, a **question and answer**.

Example 71 is a **staggered interval** descending line that provides some interesting interval leaps and accents. In bar 3, I use the C♭ (which is enharmonic to B) as a **chromatic passing tone** to the B♭ (♭7th).

Example 72 starts with a triplet pickup and then proceeds with a slowly descending repeated rhythmic figure that incorporates both the **13th (A)** and the **9th (D).** The line ends with a little blues turn.

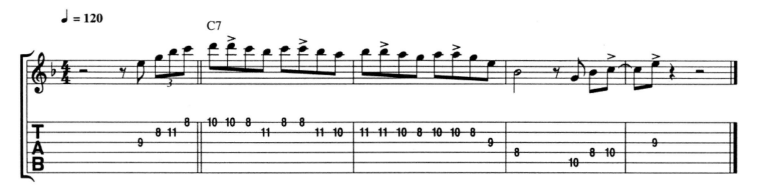

Example 73 is an arpeggio that skips the root and incorporates the ♯9 (D♯) as a bluesy approach note to the 3rd (E) and then goes to the root (C). The riff ends in some **double stops** that have a country blues flavor to them like the playing of **Jimmy Bryant.**

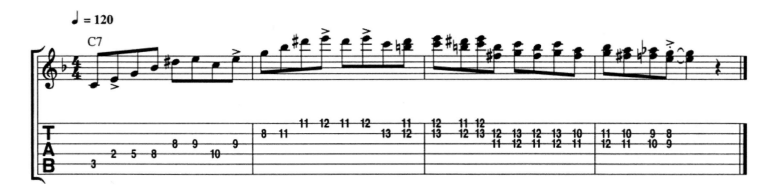

Playing on IIm7-V7-Imaj7 Changes

We have reached a point now where we can start combining and using what we have studied. With our respective Major, Dorian, and Mixolydian scales, chords, and arpeggios, we are armed to tackle the most common chord progression in the standard jazz repertoire.

The IIm7-V7-Imaj7 chord progression: We have previously played in the "key" of these changes, but we are now going to play on each separate chord change.

The 7-3 chord connection: When chords are moving in a cycle of 5ths, we can achieve smooth connection between the chords by connecting the 7th of the chord you are on to the 3rd of the chord you are going to.

Example 74 shows the connecting notes in a IIm7-V7-Imaj7 in the key of F. Notice that the 7th of the Gm7 (F) moves down a half step to the 3rd of the C7 (E). Then, the 7th of C7 (B♭) moves down a half step to the 3rd (A) of the Fmaj7 chord.

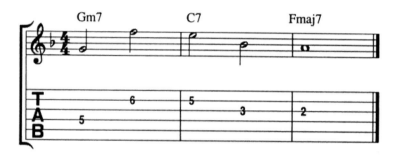

Now all we have to do is fill in the measures with notes from the scales and arpeggios from each chord change and, presto, you are playing over changes and making smooth connections between the chords.

> There are other chord connections; check them out. Do some exploring: try to connect from chord to chord by an interval no greater than a whole step.

IIm7-V7-Imaj7 Riffs

CD 21A **Example 75** makes all the connections between the chords and has two prominent features. The first is the **triplet** in bar 2. It uses the ♯9 and the ♭9. This is a classic jazz resolution to the "I" chord used by many players including alto sax great, **Charlie Parker**. The second feature in this riff is the use of the half steps between 3 and 4 and 7 and 8 in the major scale to create the descending line in bar 3.

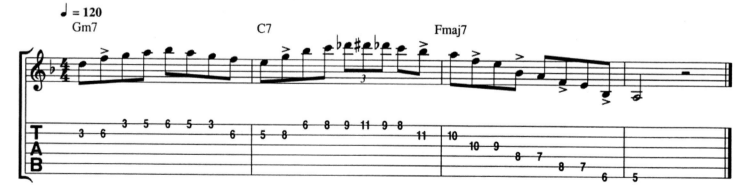

Example 76 is a triplet sequence that rests after every chord connection. It builds in pitch and resolves in the fourth bar to the major 7 note (E) of the last chord (Fmaj7).

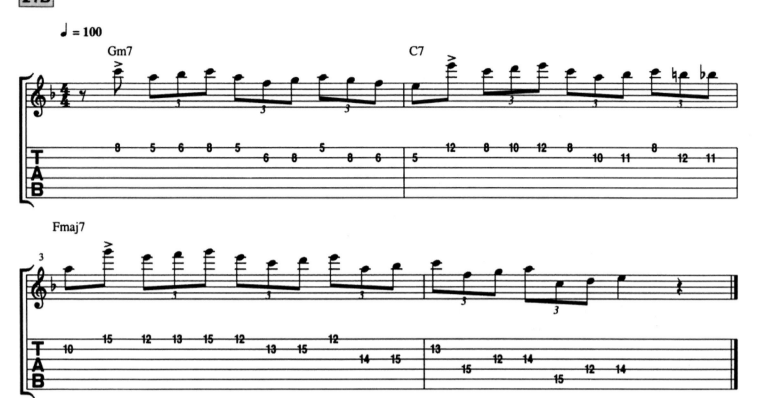

Example 77 has three sets of three chromatically descending notes that then leap down a large interval. The chord connections are really obscured because of the attention drawn by the contrasting chromatic and large interval leaps. All the chromatic notes in this example are functioning as passing tones. The riff ends on the 9th of the Fmaj7 chord.

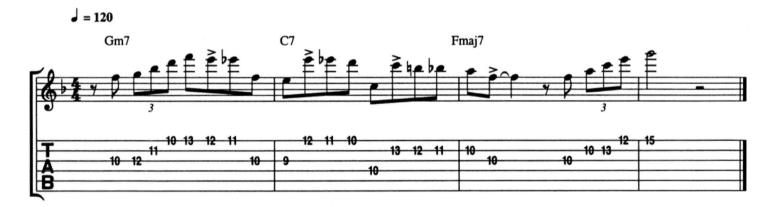

Summary Solo #5

CD 22 **Example 78** is a chord progression similar to the changes of the Thelonious Monk tune **"Well You Needn't."** The cool thing here is that all the chord changes are dominant 7. This really lets us examine the Mixolydian mode and its arpeggios. This solo is loosely based on some of the melodic ideas of "Well You Needn't."

Note:

1) The central theme to this solo is set up in bar 3. With the chords shifting by a half step, it's easy to take any ideas and just move them chromatically.

2) In bar 3 there is a chromatic approach note (G♯). In bar 5 there is a B natural played over an F7 chord. This was done to create a G triad over the F7 chord. Check out the notes G, B, and D in that bar (bar 5).

3) There is a big push into the second A section with the anticipation of the low F on the "and" of 4 in bar 8.

4) The second A section starts with a large triplet build to a descending sequence of eighth notes that continues across the chord changes and ends with the thematic riff in bars 12 and 13.

5) The B section is a study in 6ths starting with the thematic riff and then moving away from it. In bar 21 the chords keep rising but the 6ths start descending. This gives a nice contrast in motion and harmonic content over each chord.

6) The last A section continues the 6ths idea with a rather twisted reference to the melody of "Good Night Ladies."

7) The solo ends with a classic phrase using the ♭5 (C♭) and ♯9 (G♯) on the F7 chord.

Solo #5

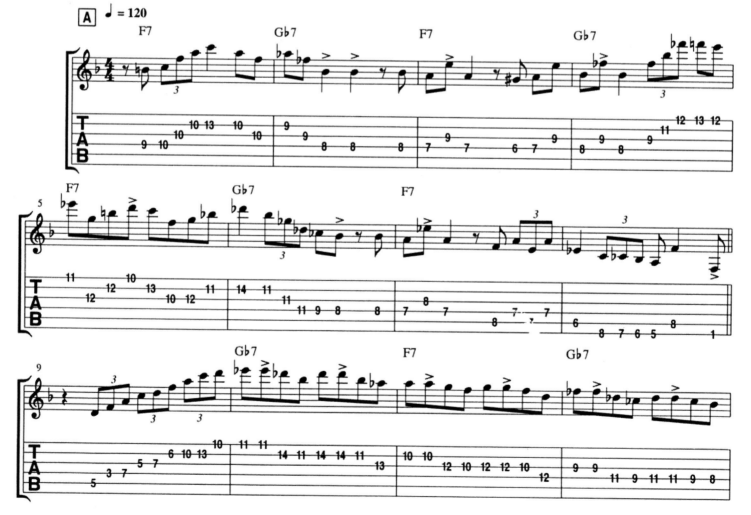

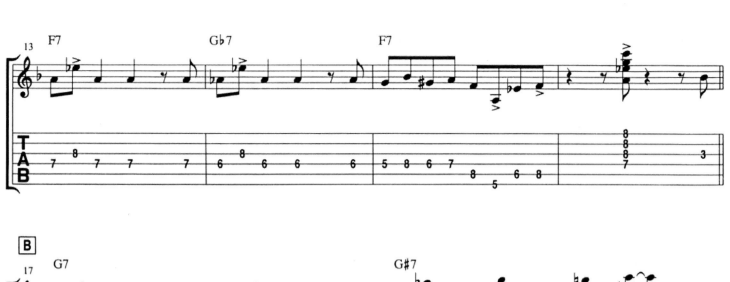

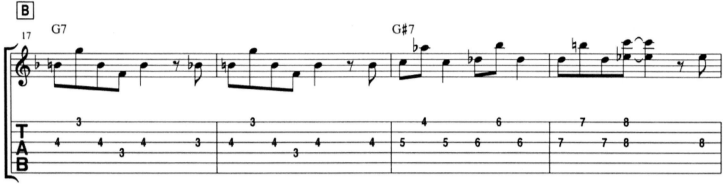

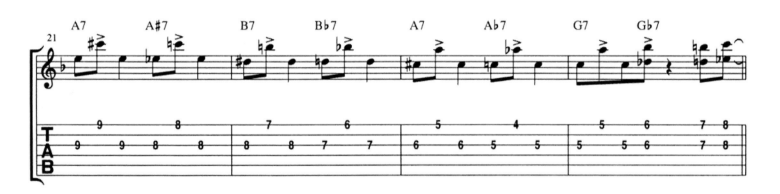

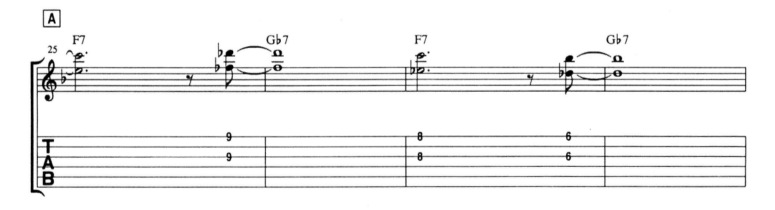

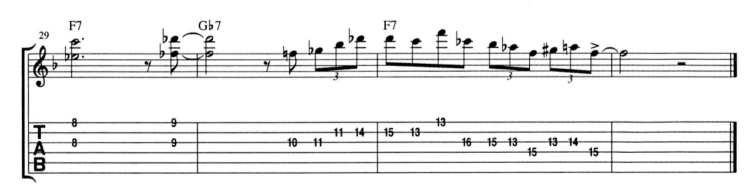

Summary Solo #6

 CD 23

Example 79 covers two choruses on chord changes similar to those of the Miles Davis composition **"Tune Up."** The two choruses are distinctly different from each other. I probably wouldn't play like this live, but I wanted to really contrast two different approaches to the chord changes.

Note:

1) The solo starts with a lot of **chromatic approach tones** in a three-bar sequence. This is followed by another sequence in bar 4 that uses non-chord tones as lower neighbor tones.

2) Bar 5 contains a commonly used chromatic descending line over a minor chord to a nice resolution on the Cmaj7 chord.

3) The first chorus ends with a sequence repeated over the last four bars (13–16).

4) The second chorus takes a different approach. Instead of running lines over each chord change, there is a single theme that is slightly altered to fit the chord changes.

5) In bar 20 there is a C natural played over the Dmaj7 chord. This anticipates the upcoming Cm7 chord.

Solo #6

54

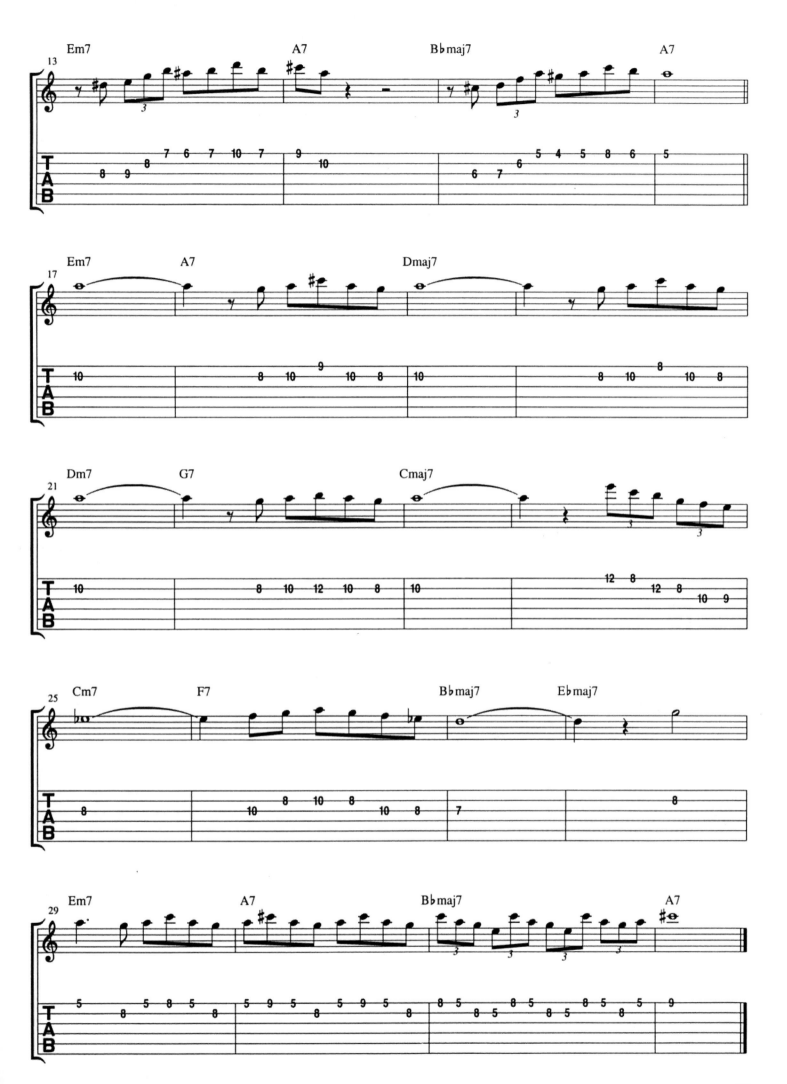

CHAPTER FOUR:
Lydian Mode [Major 7(#11) Scale]

The **Lydian mode** is a scale made up of seven notes arranged in a specific order of whole and half steps. This order originally came from the natural notes from F to F. This was the fourth of the seven Greek modes. This mode is like a major scale except that the fourth note is raised a half step. This mode can be used to play over major 7(#11) chords, and with more modern players, as a substitute for the major scale.

The arrangement of whole and half steps in the Lydian mode is W-W-W-H-W-W-H.

Example 80 shows an E♭ Lydian mode in 1st position.

I have chosen E♭ Lydian for our examples. We have looked at the key of C major, F Dorian (E♭ major), C Mixolydian (F major), and now E♭ Lydian (B♭ major). We are working a lot in flat keys because that is where most of the jazz repertoire is written—to accommodate the horn players!

Example 81 shows the E♭ Lydian mode played in every position across the fingerboard using three notes per string. Notice that in each position, I start with the root (E♭). This is to reinforce the Lydian sound.

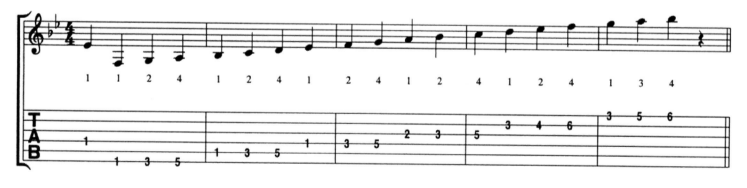

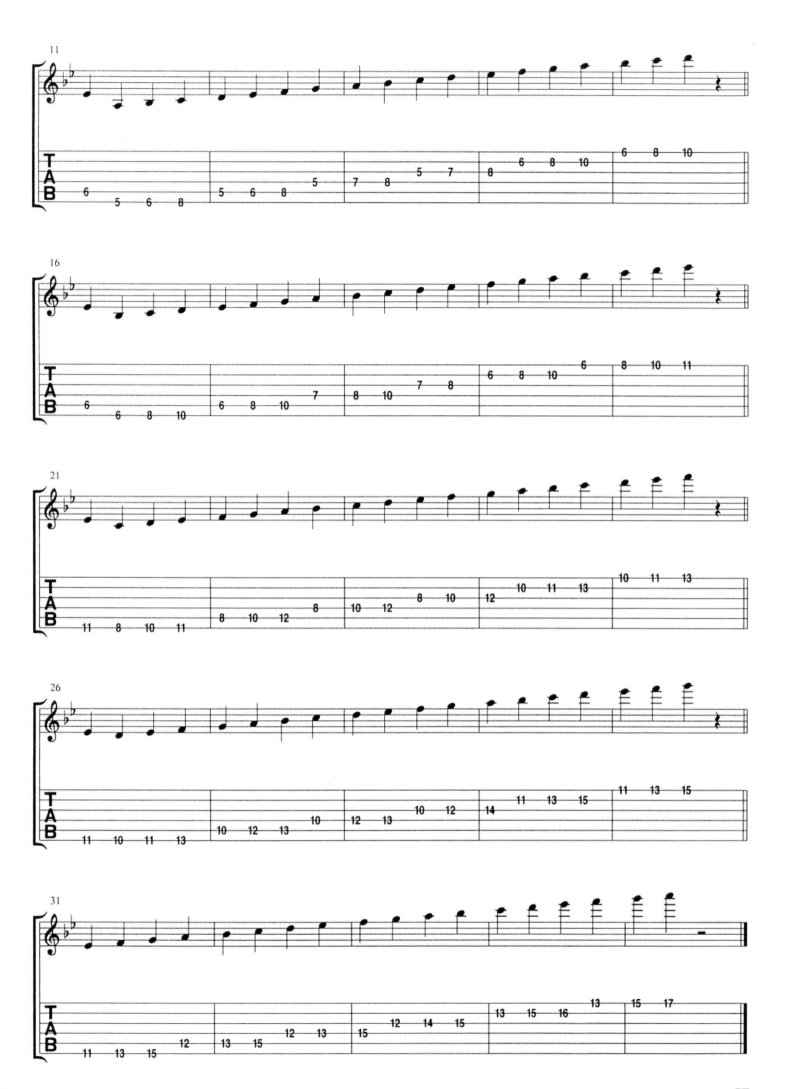

Lydian Mode Riffs

CD 24A **Example 82** is a melodic phrase loosely taken from **"The Sound of Music."** (Can you believe it?) The riff has a repeating rhythmic motif and a descending movement that is interrupted in bar 3 and then continues to resolution.

Example 83 has its origin in a line played by **John Coltrane** in the break before the start of his solo in his composition **"Moment's Notice."** The phrase repeats three times in different registers and ends with a descending triplet figure. The interesting thing about these triplets is that they are **tritones.** (The interval of the tritone equally divides the octave in half. It is a tense interval.) In the Lydian mode, the tritone is found between the root (Eb) and the raised (Lydian) 4th.

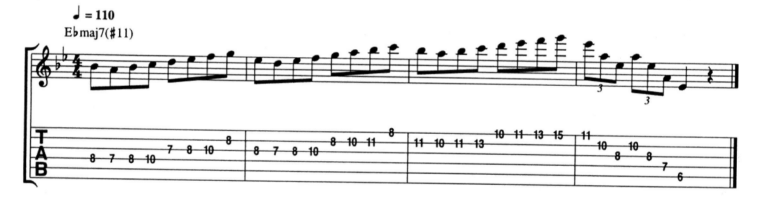

Example 84 shows how the Lydian mode is suited for playing in fourths. Pianist **McCoy Tyner** is known for his use of **quartal harmony** (playing chords built in fourths instead of thirds). This riff is the Eb Lydian mode starting on F with a note a fourth or third below preceding it. This is a beautiful sound. When you feel comfortable with this riff, try playing it using **sixteenth notes** (in all keys, of course).

Lydian Chords Major 7(#11), 9, 13

Example 85 contains some common voicings for E♭maj7(#11) chords. Explore voicings that work for you.

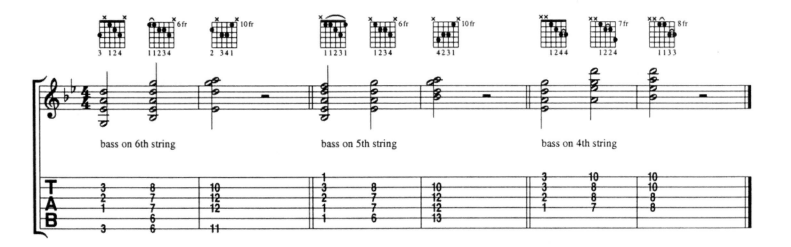

Example 86 contains some voicings that use the **Lydian 4th (A) with the 9th (F) and the 13th (C).** You will notice that when adding all of these upper extensions, we have to let a lot of the basic 1, 3, 5 of the chord go. A lot of the chord voicings in this chapter are built in fourths.

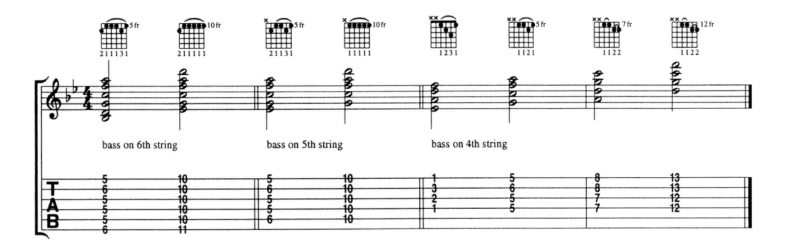

Lydian Chord Riffs

Example 87 is over a **pedal tone.** In this case we are pedaling the root (Eb). The Lydian voicings have a beautiful sound—major yet more exotic.

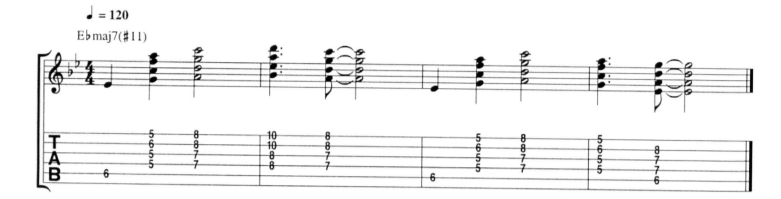

Example 88 starts with a strong Lydian sound and then descends through two **6/9 chords,** the second of which is Lydian. The riff has a strong rhythmic motif.

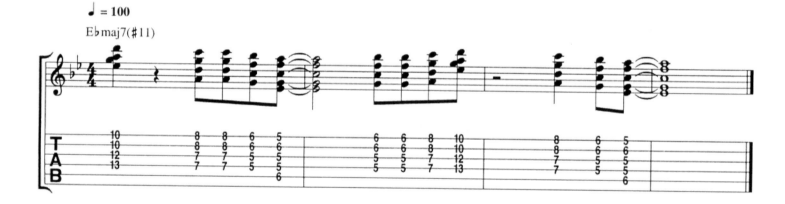

Example 89 uses a **lower neighbor chord** to move chromatically up and down in bars 2 and 4. The rhythm is in the **Wes Montgomery** style of comping and chord soloing.

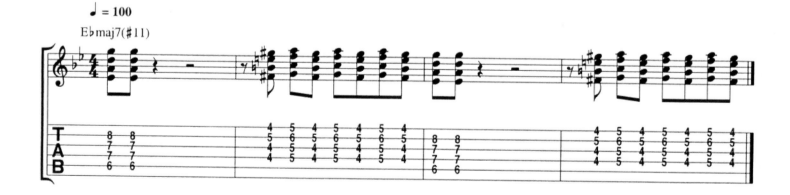

60

Major 7(#11) Arpeggios

Example 90 has some **practical fingerings** for the E♭maj7(#11) arpeggios. Check out the two half steps between 4 & 5 (A & B♭) and 7 & 8 (D & E♭). Remember: I did not repeat fingerings above the 12th fret. You should do this on your own, and practice your scales and arpeggios from the lowest to highest possible position on your guitar (in all keys, of course).

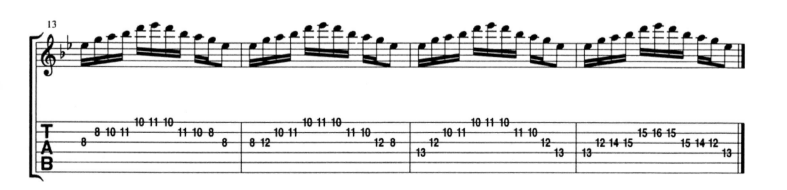

Example 91 shows the E♭maj7(♯11) arpeggio without the 5th. **The ♯11 (A) is replacing the 5th (B♭).** Technically, you would call these arpeggios E♭maj7(♭5). In these fingerings, note that I have not gone from the ♯11 (A) to the 7th (D) on the same string. If you have the fingers for that stretch, congratulations! Now go work those fingerings out for yourself.

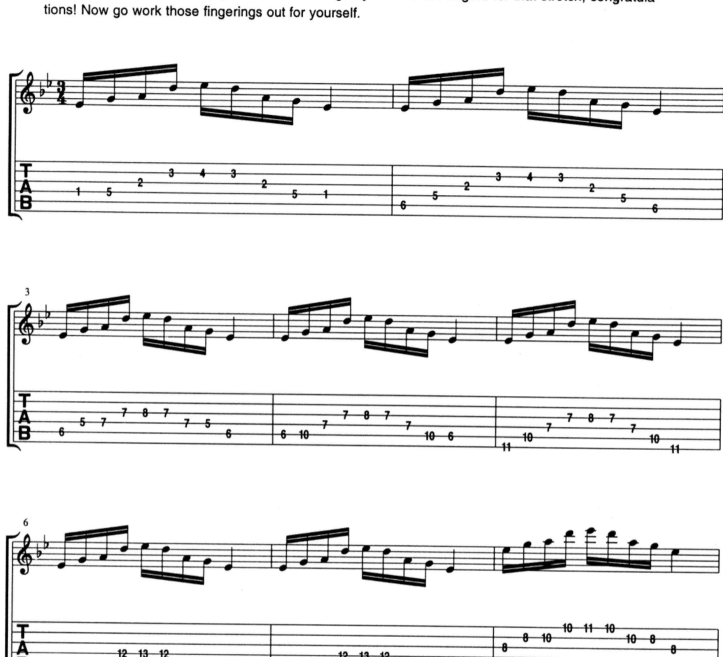

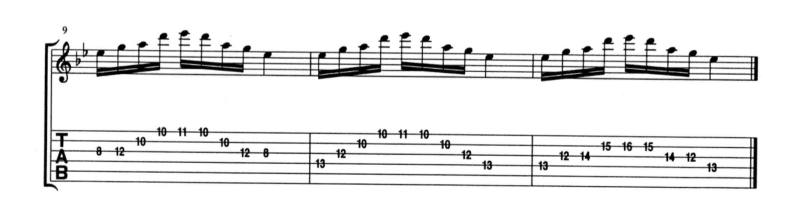

Major 7(♯11) Arpeggio Riffs

CD
26A
Example 92 has the classic ascending triplet arpeggio that is preceded by an eighth note. The rest of this riff is based on that figure. There is a big descending triplet figure in bars 3 and 4 that emphasizes the half steps in the arpeggio.

CD
26B
Example 93 is another simple figure that is displaced rhythmically in each measure. Note in bar 3 that the line comes to rest on the raised 4 (A).

CD
26C
Example 94 is showing all the 4ths that exist in this arpeggio (and a couple of 3rds). It has an Asian sound to it because of the 4ths.

Summary Solo #7

CD 27

Example 95 is based on classic Latin-jazz chord changes, similar to **Freddie Hubbard's "Little Sunflower."**

Note:

1) This song has a **bossa nova** feel: the eighth notes are straight. The theme is repeated three times and ends in a **Sonny Rollins** type of line.

2) The second A section has a rhythmic chord hit with an intervening line that exaggerates the **Dorian feel** over the D minor. It should be noted that there are not a lot of chord changes in this piece and that I am soloing on each chord change.

3) There really is no typical establishment of key in this song (no iim7-V7-I, no chord progression to suggest a key). Its what is called a **"modal" composition.**

4) In bar 12, there is a classic descending minor line. You will notice that there are lot of chord hits in this solo. Latin music is extremely rhythmic in nature (not to say that swing isn't) and lends itself to this type of playing.

5) In the first B section, we move to E♭ Lydian and the line starts on the 9th (F). **Wes Montgomery** did this a lot in his playing. The 9th (F) is emphasized for the next four bars.

6) In bar 21, the chord moves to Dmaj7(♯11), and the line sequentially builds up the **D Lydian arpeggio and mode.**

7) In the second B section, there is a sequence of four bars of mostly 6/9 chords that ends in a change back to Dmaj7(♯11) and a nice triplet figure to end the solo.

Solo #7

Summary Solo #8

 CD 28 **Example 96** is loosely based on the chord changes to Richard Rodgers' **"My Favorite Things"** from the musical **The Sound of Music.** In this piece, the solo is based mostly on the temporary key of the moment as opposed to playing on every chord change.

Note:

1) The first four bars are in the key of E minor, but check out the major 3rd (G♯) that is played in bar 2. **The major 3rd is used as a chromatic tension note** here. There is also a lot of Dorian 6th (C♯) and natural minor 6th (C). The further we go with these studies, the more you will see the use of multiple modes and arpeggios over a single chord change or tonal center. Don't forget that the chords in the first four bars are in the key of E Dorian (D major).

2) The next four bars are in the key of C Lydian. You'll notice that the same rhythmic introduction was used, but the rest of the line exploits the half steps between 7 & 8 and 4 & 5. I also threw in a half step between the ♯9th and 3rd for good measure.

3) The section ends with an exaggerated quote from "My Favorite Things."

4) Next we go to the key of E major. Our arrival is heralded by a big descending arpeggio. It's a little basic but effective. The old standby triplet riff gets us to the key of A Lydian where there is a descending scale done in a four-note sequence in an odd grouping (starting on the "and").

Solo #8

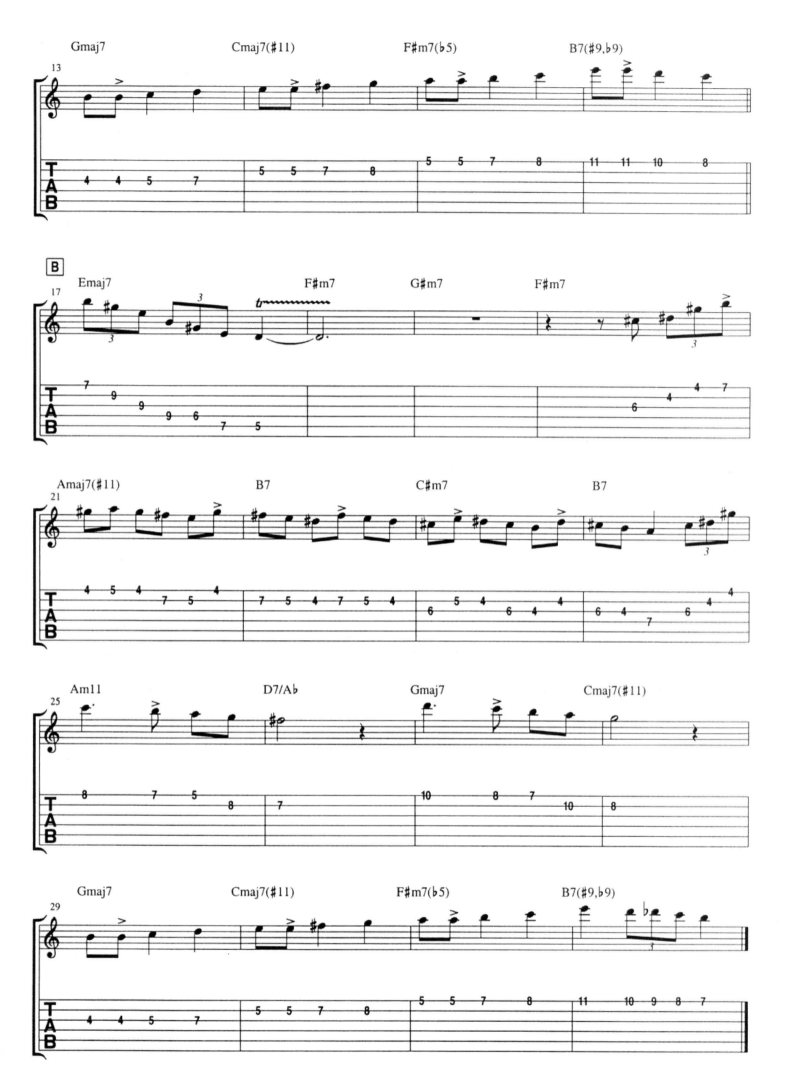

CHAPTER FIVE:
Aeolian Mode (Natural Minor Scale)

The **Aeolian mode** is a scale made up of seven notes arranged in a specific order of whole and half steps. This order originally came from the natural notes from A to A. This was the sixth of the seven Greek modes. (So the Aeolian mode [natural minor scale] is the same as a major scale beginning and ending on the sixth note.) This mode sounds minor because of the lowered third note.

The Aeolian mode, or natural minor scale, is an important theoretical structure. For every major key there is a relative minor—starting a minor 3rd down or a major 6th up from the root of the major. The scale for these minor keys is the Aeolian mode (natural minor scale), and its cousins are the harmonic minor and melodic minor scales. The harmonic and melodic minor scales are important in their own right—so important that jazz players have built modes from them.

The arrangement of whole and half steps in the Aeolian mode is W-H-W-W-H-W-W.

Example 97 shows a G Aeolian mode in 1st position.

The key signature for G Aeolian is two flats (the same as the major key of B♭). Don't forget to **practice all that you learn in this book in every key.**

Example 98 shows the G Aeolian mode played in every position across the fingerboard using three notes per string. Notice that in every position, I start with the root (G). This is to reinforce the Aeolian sound.

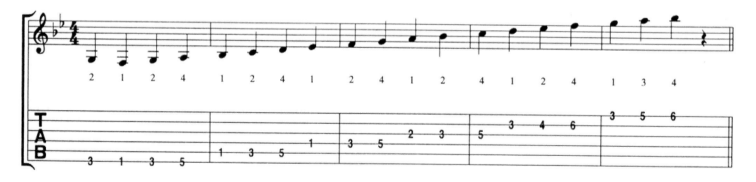

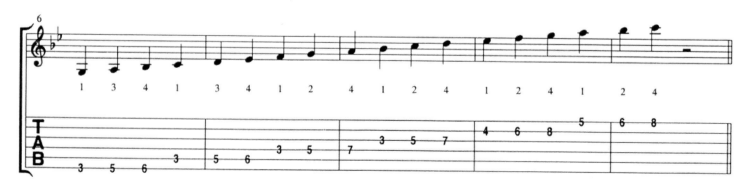

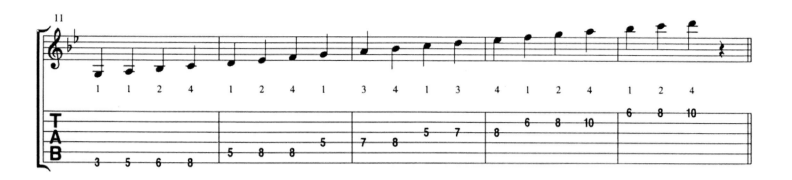

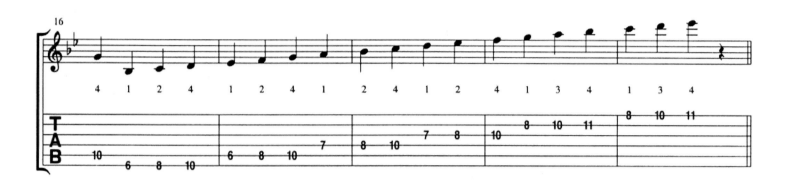

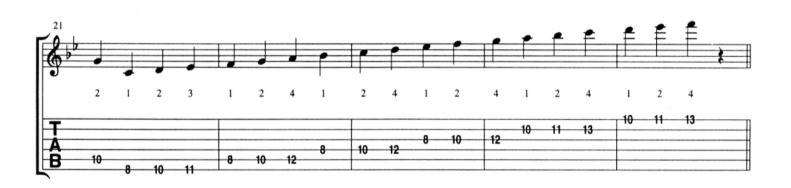

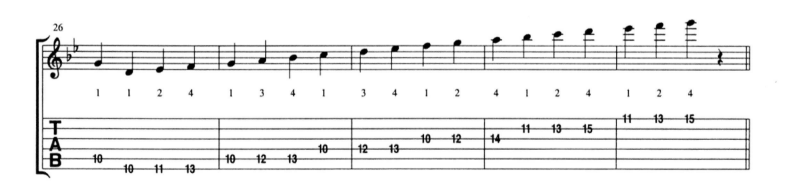

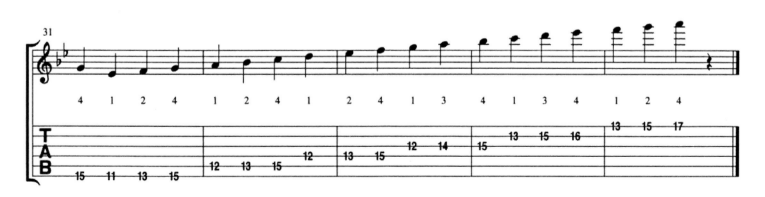

Aeolian Mode Riffs

Example 99 is a **Jim Hall**-style riff over Gm7. I am using the key signature again (B♭) to eliminate a lot of accidentals. This is pretty much a straight up and down Aeolian mode that has nice rhythmic feel and an **unexpected finish on the Aeolian 6th (E♭)**.

Example 100 is a **George Benson**-style riff starting with his trademark **octaves with a 4th in between.** This riff has a call-and-response feel to it between the triple stops and single notes.

Example 101 is a descending G Aeolian mode in 4ths starting on the 9th (A). The riff is in two parts with the same rhythmic ending.

Harmonic Minor Scale (Aeolian ♯7)

There are three forms of the minor scale: natural minor (Aeolian mode), harmonic minor, and melodic minor.

The harmonic minor scale is an Aeolian mode (natural minor scale) with a raised 7th scale degree. This gives a leading tone (major 7) to the scale. To my ear, the leading tone helps with the establishment of a V7-Im7 or "key" feel. So in jazz it's most common to find the harmonic minor used over the "five" chord in a minor key. For example, using a G harmonic minor scale over D7 helps to solidify the V7 - Im (D7 - Gm). Using a harmonic minor over a minor chord (G harmonic minor over a G minor chord) provides a dramatic, Middle Eastern quality that can be useful in some circumstances but not usually in straight-ahead jazz.

The order of whole and half steps is W-H-W-W-H-W-H-H.

There are modes made from the harmonic minor scale. We will look only at the basic scale here.

Example 102 is a one-octave G harmonic minor scale in 1st position.

Example 103 shows the G harmonic minor scale played in every possible position across the fingerboard using three notes per string. Notice that in every position, I start with the root (G). This is to reinforce the Aeolian sound. Remember: All modes are scales but not all scales are modes. The harmonic minor scale was derived from the Aeolian mode.

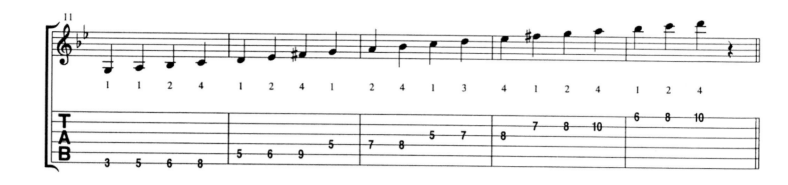

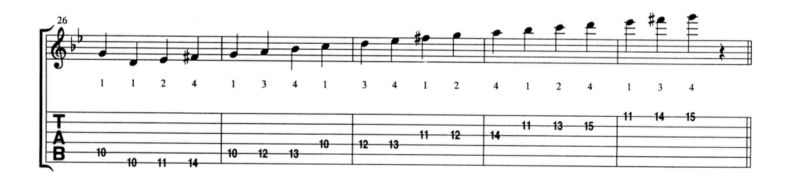

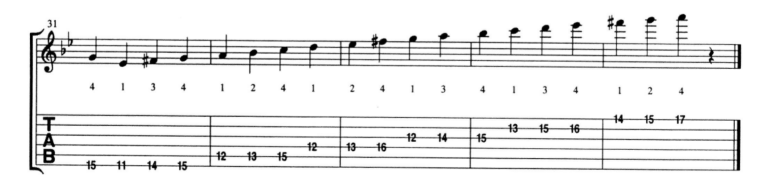

Harmonic Minor Scale Riffs

 Example 104 is a **Pat Martino** type of riff. Bar 1 pedals the major 7 (F#) and then launches upward. Bar 3 has some cool **"crushed tone" double stops.** The riff ends in bar 4 with a classic blues line.

 Example 105 explores the Bb augmented major 7 chord that exists in the G harmonic minor scale (Bb, D, F#, A). This riff starts on an off beat, which increases its urgent sound. Notice that the accents here are on the beats. This is basically a sequential riff except for the finger stretch to the D in bar 2.

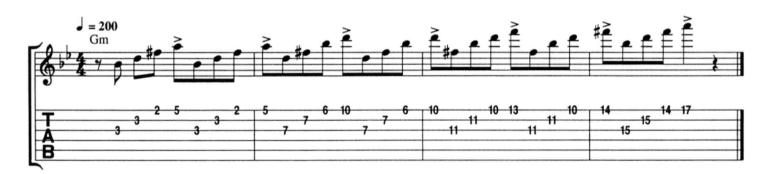

 Example 106 is pretty much straight out of the **Johann Sebastian Bach** book. It has two classical-style sequences: the first starting after the pickup bar and the second in bar 3. Bach had some swinging lines, baby!

Harmonic Minor (maj7) Chords

In Chapter Two we looked at minor and minor 7 chords. Instead of repeating that here for the Aeolian mode, I thought we would do the minor (maj7) chords for the harmonic minor scale.

Example 107 shows some common fingerings for Gm(maj7) chords. Check out all the **augmented triads** created in inversions when we omit the root! (F♯aug, B♭aug, and Daug triads)

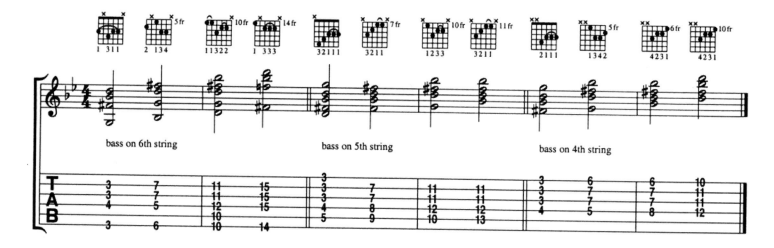

Harmonic Minor (maj7) Chord Riffs

Example 108 is a **bossa nova**-style chord vamp. A lot of Latin rhythms are two-bar-long repeated phrases. That is what happens here. There is a little extra payoff in bar 4 with the higher inversion on the last two hits. Trumpet great **Dizzy Gillespie** was among the first to introduce Latin and Afro-Cuban music to jazz.

Example 109 is a slow swing riff. Notice that in the first two bars, the rhythm is **square,** or on the beat. This sets up for the rhythmic syncopation in bars 3 and 4. This riff is a little tricky to execute, so take your time and don't get frustrated. Keep working at it and you'll get it. Don't forget the key signature!

Example 110 is an **up-tempo combination chord and single-note riff.** The line descends across the four bars. Chords and single notes are traded off.

Harmonic Minor (maj7) Arpeggios

Again, instead of duplicating the minor and minor 7 arpeggios from our Dorian chapter, we will take a look at the harmonic minor arpeggios.

Example 111 has some fingerings for one-octave harmonic minor arpeggios. Some of the fingerings may seem a bit awkward, but I wanted to stretch some of the possibilities. Now it's your turn to take these and combine them to form two- and three-octave arpeggios.

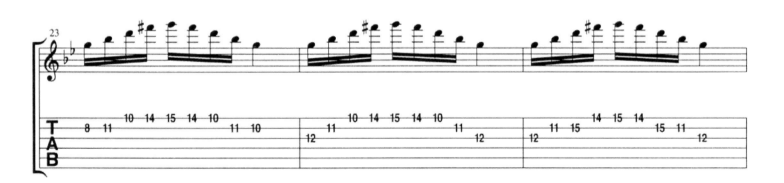

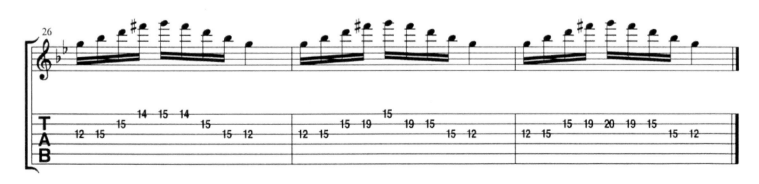

Harmonic Minor (maj7) Arpeggio Riffs

CD 32A **Example 112** is a **Barney Kessel**-style riff. Barney used the harmonic minor arpeggio in his compositions as well as in his soloing. In bar 2, the riff lands on the **9th (A).** The riff ends with a line showing the half steps in the harmonic minor scale (2 & 3 and 7 & 8).

CD 32B **Example 113** is a three-octave arpeggio run with a melodic reference to **"Billy's Bounce"** in bar 2, which ends up on the ♭7 (F natural) in bar 3. The riff ends with a lower chromatic approach note to each note in a descending G minor triad (D, B♭, G).

CD 32C **Example 114** is a ballad riff in the style of **"Round Midnight."** It has a sad and bluesy feel to it. Notice the contrasting note lengths and rests.

Aeolian (Natural Minor) Scale Tone Chords

The Aeolian mode and its derivative key signatures are relative to the Ionian, or major, scale. We looked at the scale tone chords in major; now we will construct the scale tone chords for its relative minor (Aeolian) scale.

Example 115 is the scale tone chords for G minor. You will notice that we used the key signature for G minor, which is relative to B♭ major. What I have done is written a G Aeolian mode and then built up a four-note chord in 3rds above each note. You will notice that we used a non-diatonic note (F♯) on the five chord (D7). This is done to make it a dominant 7 instead of a minor 7. **The D7 establishes the key of G minor with the leading tone (F♯).** Here is an example of the harmonic minor scale in action: The F♯, or raised 7, gives the major 3rd of the five chord and helps establish a key feel as opposed to a modal feel. You will see that the result is a series of major 7, minor 7, dominant 7, and minor 7(♭5) chords. Again, notice that these are written theoretically. These are not guitar voicings!

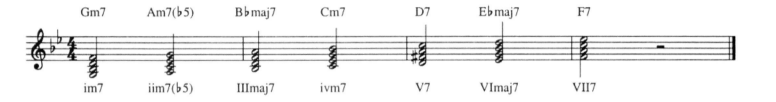

Just like our major scale tone chords, this sequence of chord types will be the same in every key. We use Roman numerals to identify the chords; this way, we can play a specific chord progression in any key [for example, iim7(♭5)-V7-im7].

Memorize the minor scale tone chords and work on them as you did the major scale tone chords.

Summary Solo #9

Example 116 is based on the chord changes to the bossa nova-style song, "Black Orpheus."

Note:

1) The first three bars flip back and forth between natural and harmonic minor. I am pretty much playing in the key of A minor as opposed to playing over each chord change.

2) In bar 4, I play a B half-diminished arpeggio. We will cover that in the next chapter; think of it as a preview of what's coming in Chapter Six.

3) The next three bars (6, 7, 8) feature some arpeggios and a chromatic line. Here I do play on each chord change.

4) Letter B starts a giant melodic sequence that runs through the entire section. Chromatic notes are used to make a smooth transition between chord changes.

5) At the end of the phrase, I leave an entire bar open. I do this a few times in this solo. **The use of space is as important as your use of notes.**

6) The last A section starts with an emulation of a false fingering riff played by saxophonists. You will see in bar 17 that there are three E's played in a row, but they are played on two different strings. This gives a slightly different timbre to the same note as it is played on two strings of different thickness.

7) In bar 20, there is a sequential diatonic ascending line with a descending chromatic "answer" in the following bar.

8) Bar 22 has an F natural note on an A7 chord. This creates an augmented feel (more on this in Chapter Seven).

9) Bar 23 is a little line highlighting the half steps in harmonic minor on the Dm7 chord. (Can you play a major 7 on a minor 7 chord? Yes!)

10) The C section is a re-creation of the line played in the B section except it's over different changes.

Solo #9

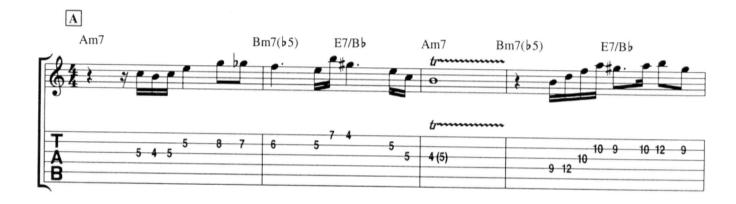

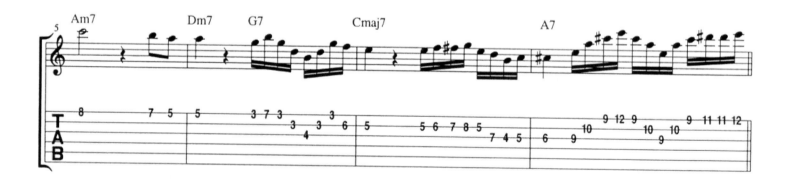

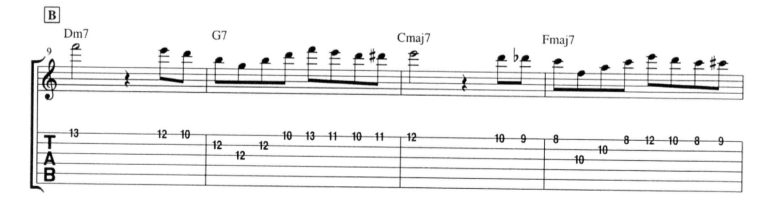

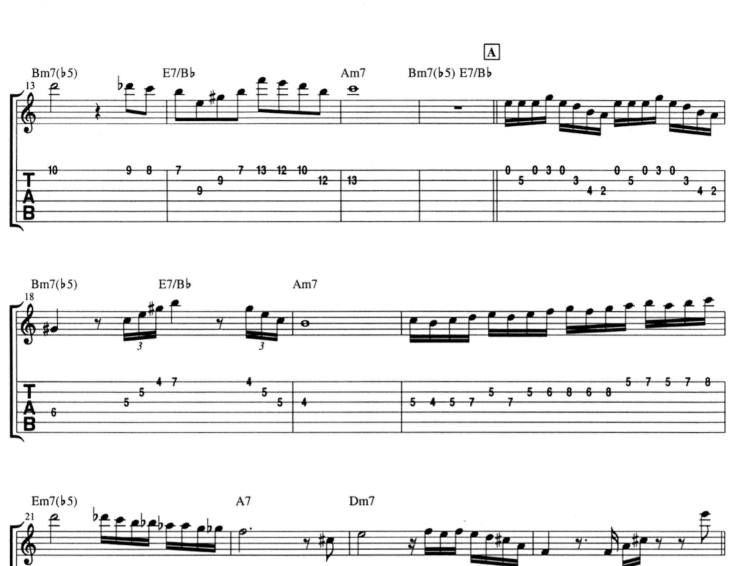

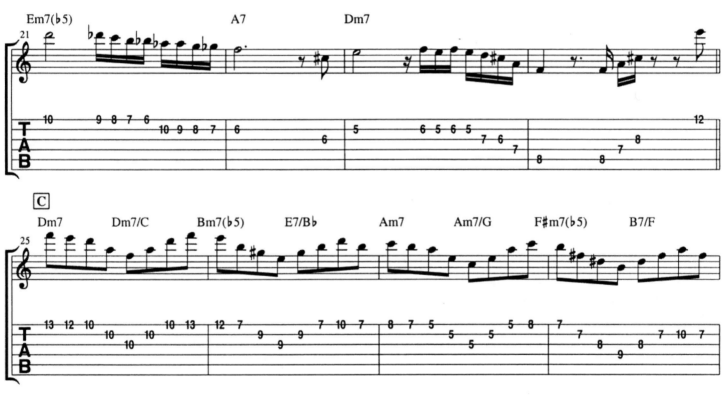

Summary Solo #10

CD
34

Example 117 has a bluesy feel to it. The chord changes are similar to those of Dennis and Brent's "Angel Eyes."

Note:

1) There is a pickup riff into bar 1 that is followed by a series of standard minor lines ending with a C harmonic minor riff that emphasizes the ♭9 (A♭) of the V7 chord (G7).

2) The first A section ends with a riff played in two different octaves. The second A section emphasizes the A♭7 chord in bar 11 by outlining its arpeggio.

3) By using notes from the C harmonic minor scale over the G7 chord in bar 13, we create an augmented (♯5) sound.

4) The end of the second A section has a **Wes Montgomery**-style riff with a subtle chromatic change that anticipates the next section.

5) The B section starts off with a sequential line that runs through the chord changes.

6) In bar 21, we start a progression of chords beneath a pedal tone (C), which eventually starts moving to support the changing harmonies.

7) The last A section starts with a big arpeggio in bar 26 and a restating of a riff from the beginning in bars 27 and 28.

8) Bar 29 is a G arpeggio that leads to the last line, which is a twisted paraphrase of the melody from **Roland Kirk's "Serenade to a Cuckoo"**—go figure.

Solo #10

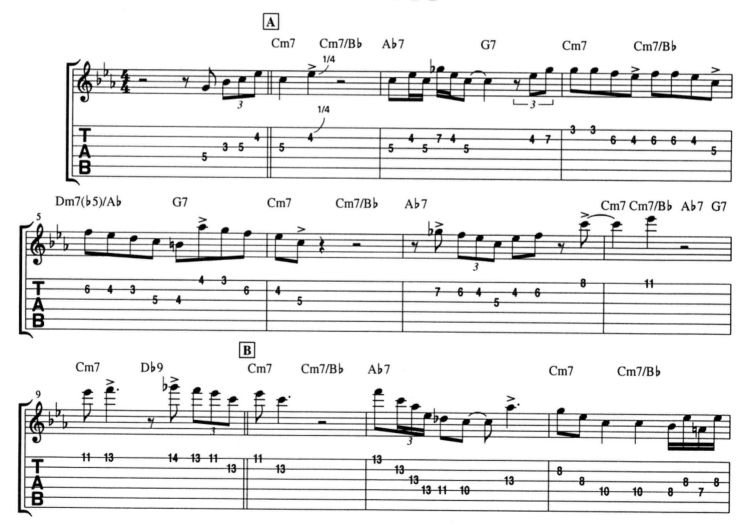

CHAPTER SIX:
Locrian Mode (Half-Diminished Scale)

The Locrian mode is the seventh of the Greek modes. It is based on the natural notes from B to B. The chord that it is associated with it is the minor 7(♭5) or half-diminished chord. As you will see, the Locrian mode is an essential ingredient in minor ii-V playing.

The arrangement of whole and half steps in the Locrian mode is H-W-W-H-W-W-W.

Example 118 shows an E Locrian mode in 1st position.

The key signature for E Locrian is one flat (B♭), the same as F major. Practice everything you learn through the cycle of 5ths.

Example 119 shows the E Locrian mode played in every position across the fingerboard using three notes per string. Notice that in every position, I start with the root (E). Again, this is to reinforce the Locrian sound. There are other common fingerings for scales, but I have picked the three-note-per-string type because I feel it gets you to play more horizontally as opposed to vertically across the neck.

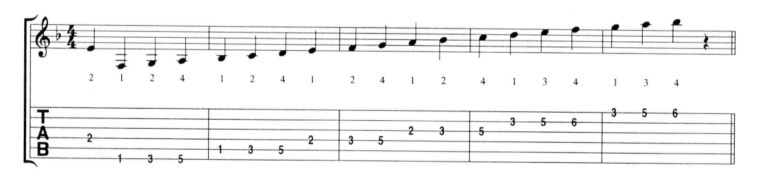

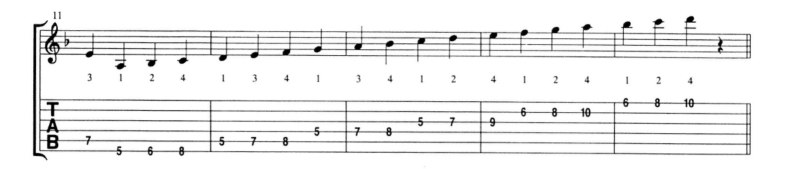

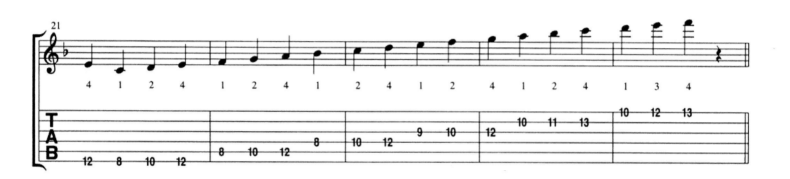

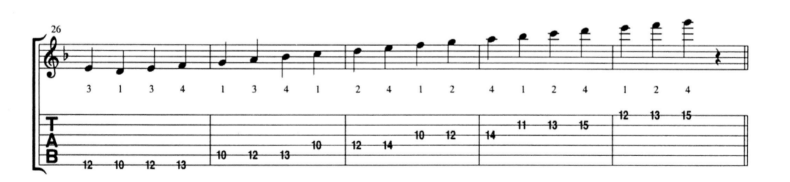

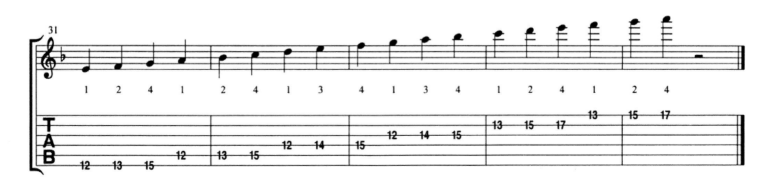

Locrian Mode Riffs

CD
35A

Example 120 is a two-part riff that emphasizes the root (E). Don't forget the key signature.

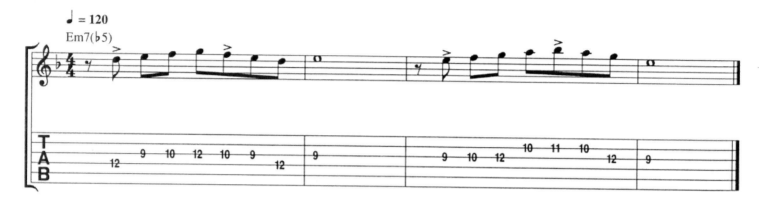

CD
35B

Example 121 is a **diatonic descending four-note sequence** that starts with three notes to throw it off the beat. The riff ends in bar 4 with a little blues turn.

CD
35C

Example 122 starts with a **pedal type of riff** off the root (E). Bar 2 is a blues-style line with a chromatic passing note (D♯). Bar 3 is an answer to bar 2 and ends with a resolution to the tonic (E).

Minor 7(♭5) Chords (Half-Diminished Chords)

Minor 7(♭5) chords sound a little weird by themselves. It is an unstable sounding chord. The ♭5 is just waiting to resolve to the root of its V chord. (For example, the B♭ of the Em7(♭5) wants to move down by a half step to the root of the A7 chord.)

Example 123 shows some fingerings for Em7(♭5) chords. Some voicings are tough, but I wanted to include all the inversions on the 6th, 5th, and 4th strings. Remember: I'm using a key signature.

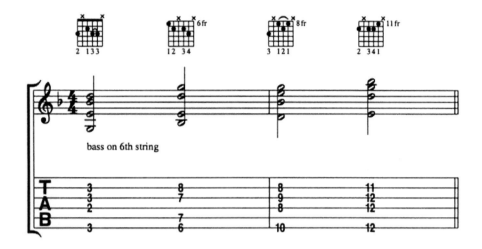

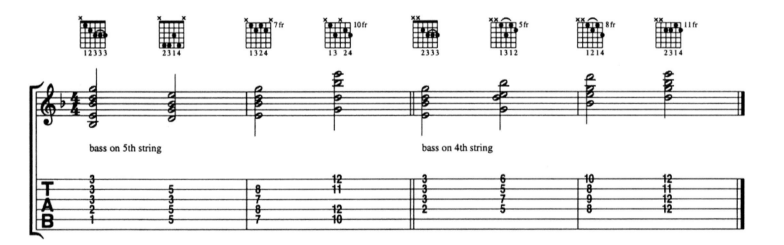

Minor 7(♭5) Chord Riffs

Now, I can't recall a song where I've had to sit on a half-diminished chord for four bars. But here are some four-bar riffs just in case.

Example 124 is a rather dense eight-note riff with some **diatonic single notes** thrown in to help the chords move. There is a definite sequential pattern to this riff.

Example 125 takes advantage of the open E string. There is a rhythmic pattern that is repeated between the chords and the open low E. In bar 4, I do a little chromatic move by raising the entire voicing a half step.

Example 126 is a riff made up of two classic rhythms: the first is in bar 1 and the other is in bar 3. This is a rather basic feel, but very effective.

Minor 7(♭5) Arpeggios

Example 127 shows some fingerings for one-octave half-diminished arpeggios. As usual, I haven't repeated fingerings above the 12th fret. Please combine these to form your own two- and three-octave arpeggios—in every key.

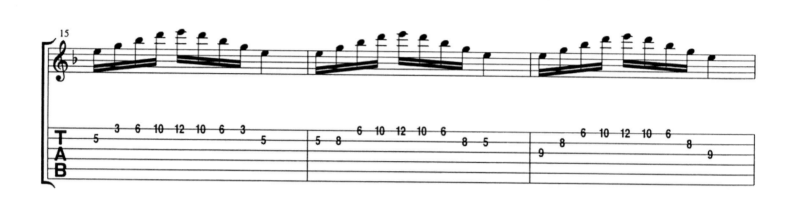

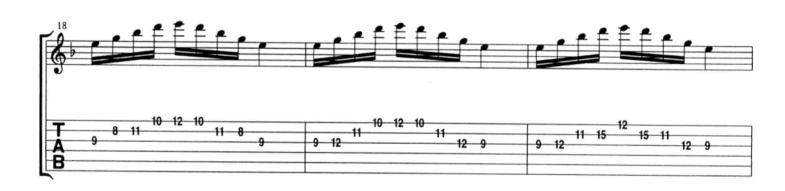

Minor 7(♭5) Arpeggios Riffs

 Example 128 is a **two-bar rhythmic phrase** that increases in intensity in bar 3. Bars 2 and 4 use the same rhythm and the same **tritone,** just inverted.

 Example 129 is a shorter **one-bar phrase** that is basically repeated three times and then resolved, or "answered," in bar 4.

 Example 130 is a two-octave arpeggio in a **repeated two-note sequence** with a little rhythmic payoff in bar 4. Notice the **tritone** in bar 4.

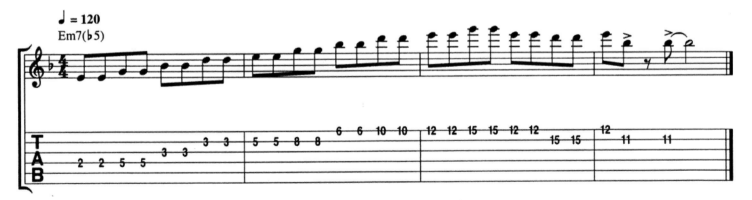

Minor ii-V-i (iim7♭5-V7-im7) Chord Connections

With the addition of the Locrian mode and its chords and arpeggios, we are now ready to play on each chord change in a minor ii-V-i. Besides the **7-3 chord connection** we talked about in Chapter Three (the 7th of the ii chord resolves down a half step to the 3rd of the V7 chord), we will look at another smooth chord connection, the **♭5-1 connection** between the iim7(♭5) and the V7 chord.

Example 131 shows the connecting notes in a iim7(♭5)-V7-Im7 in the key of D minor. Notice that the 7th of the Em7(♭5) (D) moves down a half step to the 3rd of the A7 (C♯). Then, the 7th of A7 (G) moves down a whole step to the 3rd (F) of the Dm7 chord.

Example 132 shows the option of the ♭5-1 connection. Notice that the ♭5 of Em7(♭5) (B♭) moves down a half step to the root of the A7 chord (A). Then, the 7th of A7 (G) moves down a whole step to the 3rd (F) of the Dm7 chord.

Minor ii-V-i (iim7(♭5)-V7-im7) Riffs

Example 133 is a riff that uses chord tones. This example highlights the **7-3 chord connection** between the iim7(♭5) and the V7. In bars 3 and 4 there is a **lower chromatic approach note** used to precede each chord tone. **Jim Hall** is one player among many who uses this technique.

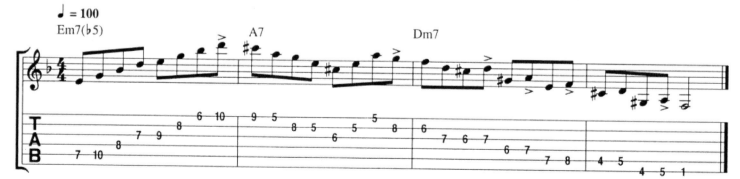

CD
38B
Example 134 uses the ♭5-1 **connection** between the iim7(♭5) (Em7(♭5)) and the V (A7). Bar 1 is a **descending sequence of E Locrian scale tones.** Bar 2 is an **A7 arpeggio with the ♭9** (B♭) on top. The riff ends with a **triplet arpeggio** and then a final D note in bar 4.

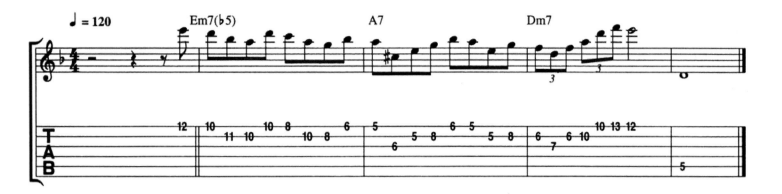

CD
38C
Example 135 has yet another chord connection, **the 5-1,** on the iim7(♭5) (Em7(♭5)) going to the V7 (A7). Bar 1 is an odd-grouped Locrian sequence in triplets that moves to the A7 in bar 2 and continues the triplets across the bar line. Then the riff smoothes out to eighth notes just in time to bring a different feel in bars 3 and 4 with the **eighth- and sixteenth-note combo minor pentatonic line.** This riff is a clash of different styles. **McCoy Tyner** employs the use of contrasting styles at the same time in his playing.

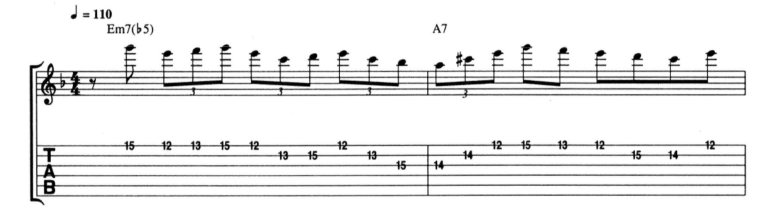

93

Summary Solo #11

Example 136 is based on chord changes similar to **"Stella by Starlight."** Throughout this entire solo, check out all the different chord connections.

Note:

1) The first A section starts out with a small melodic quote and then proceeds with short repetitive **Sonny Rollins**-like riffs.

2) In bar 7, the line sits on the ♯11 (A) and then does a little arpeggio that neatly moves to the A♭7 chord. In this solo, I am definitely playing on each chord change.

3) Letter B continues with the Sonny Rollins-style lines. Bars 11 and 12 are the same riff played in **sequence, a minor 3rd apart** (that's how I justify the G natural on the D♭9 chord).

4) Bar 14 goes to the key of F major, going down the scale in 6ths. We do, however, accommodate the E♭9 chord with a D♭ in the line in bar 15.

5) In the C section, there is a **sequence of triads** that are found in the chord changes. They are moving up or down by whole or half steps. If you look at your scales, arpeggios, and chords, you will find that other harmonies exist within them.

6) The last section is a giant sequence of **Wes Montgomery**-style octaves that ends in a blues riff.

Solo #11

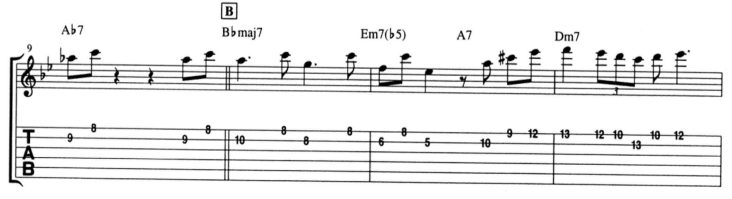

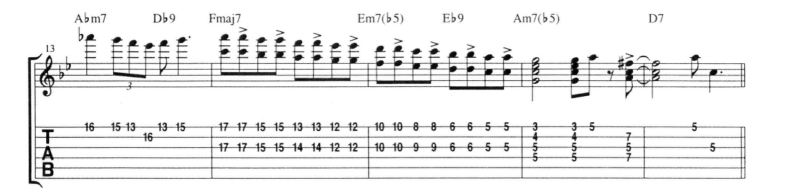

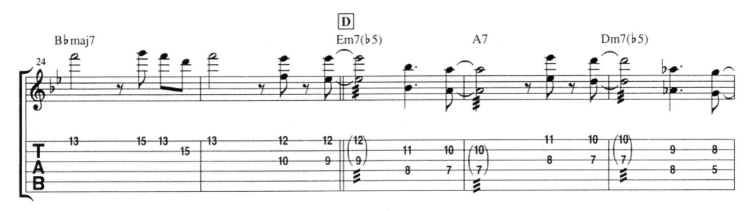

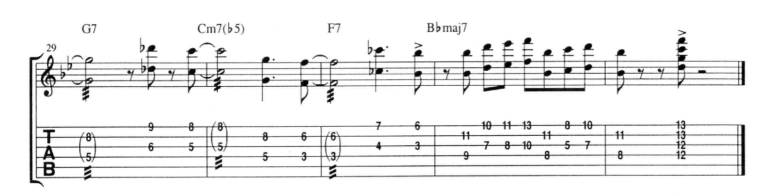

Summary Solo #12

CD 40 **Example 137** is based on changes similar to Cole Porter's "Night and Day."

Note:

1) The solo starts with a combination arpeggio and chromatic line.
2) Bars 4 and 5 use a C Aeolian mode and then switch to the harmonic minor over the G7. This is followed in bar 7 by a diatonic triplet riff with **displaced octaves** in the style of guitarist **Joe Diorio.**
3) Letter C uses double stops that are almost country sounding. Next we have some double stops that are mostly Lydian 4ths with a couple of 3rds thrown in (bars 21 and 22).
4) The solo winds down with a classic old-style riff and some 6/9 chords.

Solo #12

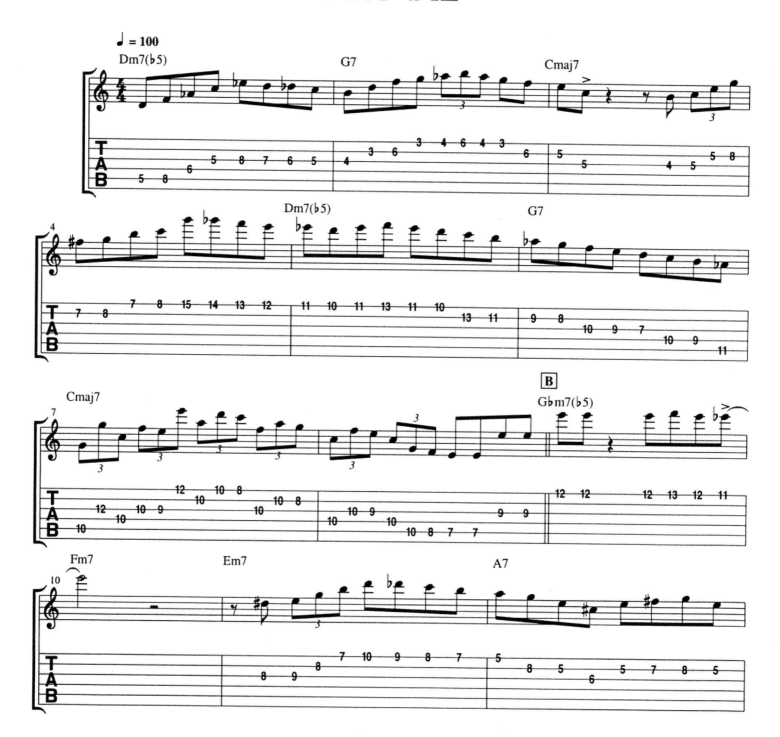

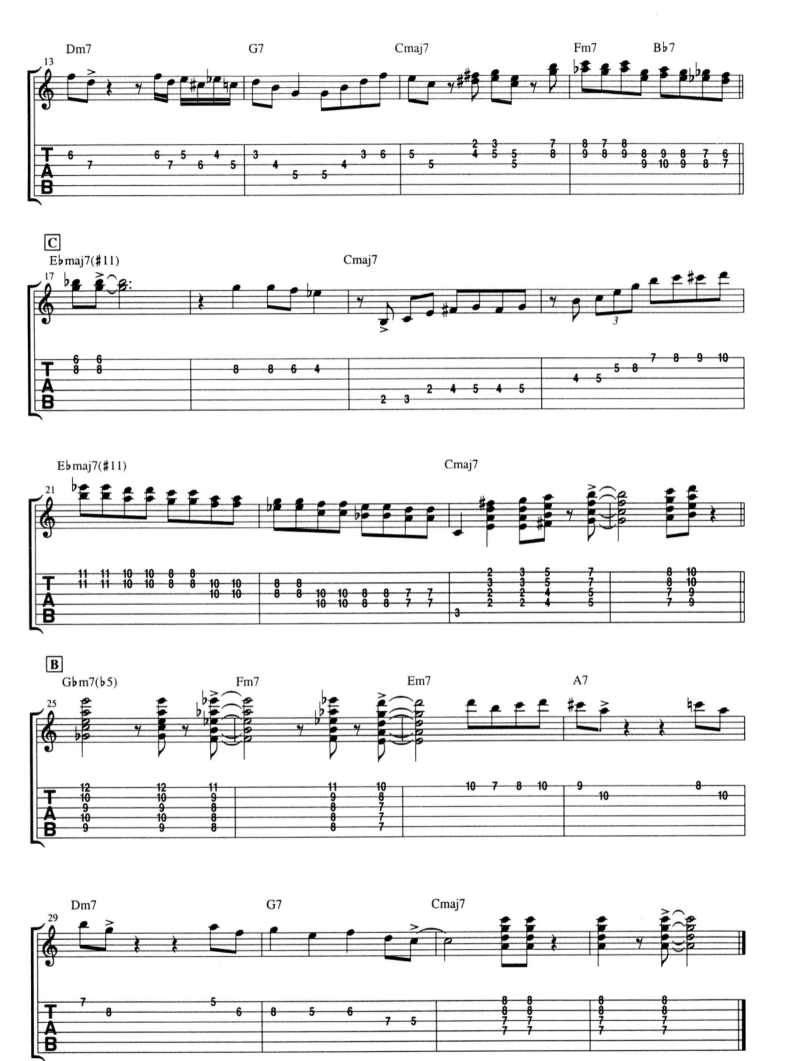

CHAPTER SEVEN:
Whole Tone Scale

The whole tone scale is *not* one of the seven Greek modes. It is a six-note scale in which every note is a whole step apart. It is mostly used over dominant 7 chords with a raised or lowered 5th. You can also use it over minor chords to get a weird "altered minor" sound. When doing this, you are really just superimposing the augmented V7 chord of whatever minor chord you are on.

The arrangement of whole steps in the whole tone scale is W-W-W-W-W-W.

Example 138 shows a C whole tone scale in 1st position.

There is no key signature for the C whole tone scale. The closest thing would be to think of a C whole tone scale as a C Mixolydian mode with a raised 4th and 5th degree. If we do that, then we would use the key of one flat (C Mixolydian or F major).

Example 139 shows some fingerings for the C whole tone scale. I am going to stray from the purely three-notes-per-string fingerings we've been doing up until now. The whole tone scale has the same fingering starting on any note in the scale. (This is because all the notes are the same distance apart.) So I am going to write down some other types of fingerings other than just three notes per string.

Whole Tone Scale Riffs

Example 140 is a riff that alternates between eighth notes and eighth-note triplets. It also emphasizes the "and" of beat 4 every other bar.

Example 141 is a little riff that keeps getting moved back one beat in each successive bar until it gets back to where it started in bar 4. This is an example of a **rhythmic sequence** more than a melodic or harmonic sequence.

Example 142 is a classic phrase used a lot by horn players (though not exclusively). In bar 3, I cheat a little because I use an F natural to resolve to the E in bar 4. Sometimes you just have to go with what you feel sounds best.

Whole Tone Chords
[Augmented, Dom7(#5/♭5)]

Example 143 shows the basic C augmented triad in every inversion on the 6th, 5th, and 4th strings.

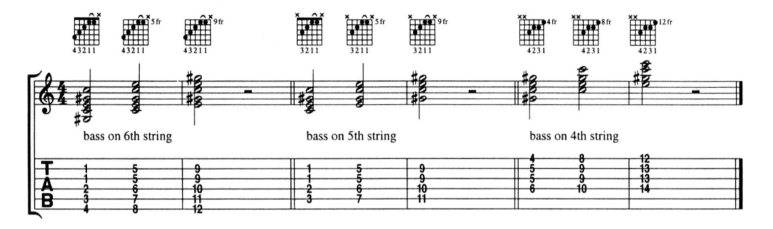

Example 144 adds the dominant 7 (B♭) to the C augmented triad. We now can show four different inversions of the chord on the 6th, 5th, and 4th strings.

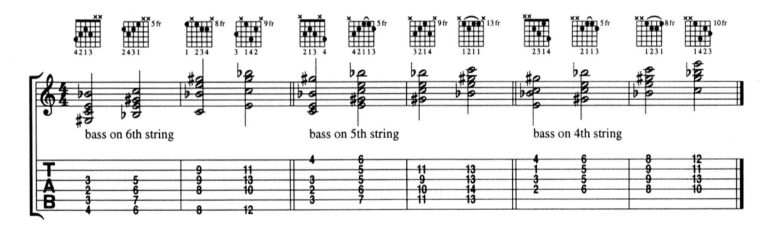

Example 145 is a C dominant 7(♭5) chord in all of its inversions on the 6th, 5th, and 4th strings.

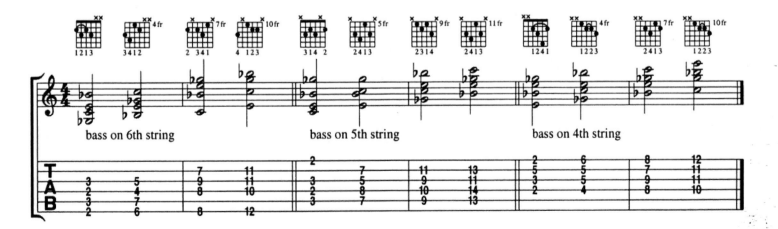

Whole Tone Chord
[Augmented, Dom7(#5/b5)] Riffs

 Example 146 is a riff based on the C augmented triad. It's played with groups of three notes in a **rhythmic and melodic sequence.**

 Example 147 is out of the **Thelonious Monk** book of quirky rhythmic chords. There is a sequence of single notes and chords with two different rhythmic payoffs in bars 2 and 4.

 Example 148 uses a sequence of alternating long and short notes in a **syncopated pattern.** The top note of each chord voicing creates a temporary melodic line.

Augmented Triad Arpeggios

Example 149 shows some fingerings for one-octave C augmented triads. Don't forget to combine these into two- and three-octave arpeggios—in all keys!

Augmented Triad Arpeggio Riffs

CD

43A
Example 150 is a two-bar **antecedent** phrase followed by a two-bar **consequent** phrase (question and answer or call and response). The riffs are a mixture of triplets and eighth notes. Note that the lines start off the beat and go across the bar line.

CD

43B
Example 151 is a syncopated riff that has an interesting fingering pattern. I played the first two bars of the riff on the 2nd and 3rd strings so I would be in position for the three-note sequence in bars 3 and 4.

CD

43C
Example 152 uses the lower chromatic approach note to a series of double stops: each diatonic double stop is preceded by a chromatic double stop a half step below. In bar 3, the line opens up with a two-octave arpeggio and then ends in the upper register.

Augmented Dominant 7 Arpeggios

Example 153 shows some fingerings for a one-octave C7(♯5) arpeggio. Check out the three whole steps at the top of the arpeggio (♯5, ♭7, 1 or G♯, B♭, C).

Augmented Dominant 7 Arpeggio Riffs

CD **44A** **Example 154** is a riff based on the whole steps between the ♯5, ♭7, and root in an augmented 7th arpeggio. The riff is staggered to lend syncopation to the overall line.

CD **44B** **Example 155** uses the ♭7 (B♭) sparingly in bars 2 and 4. The riff is stated in bars 1 and 2, and then it is inverted (sort of) in bars 3 and 4.

CD **44C** **Example 156** is an old-style **Django Reinhardt** type of riff. Notice the B naturals (the major 7th) in bars 2 and 4. Think of them as a **chromatic approach** note to the C or a **lower neighbor** tone to the C.

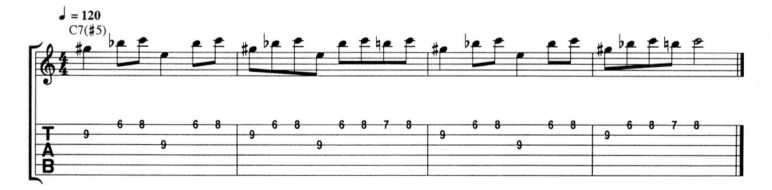

Dominant 7(♭5) Arpeggios

Example 157 shows a variety of fingerings for one-octave C7(♭5) arpeggios. Notice that there are some pretty wide finger stretches because of the distance between the ♭5 and ♭7 (major 3rd).

Dominant 7(♭5) Arpeggio Riffs

CD 45A **Example 158** has a bluesy quality to it. It's a short motif that is repeated with a payoff in bar 4.

CD 45B **Example 159** sounds like some kind of demented **Henry Mancini** line—like the "Peter Gunn" theme but a little more scary. This riff is really just straight up the arpeggio with a little rhythmic motif.

CD 45C **Example 160** uses the **tritone** between the ♭5 (G♭) and the root (C). There are some wide interval leaps here and some **string skipping** in bar 3.

Summary Solo #13

CD 46 Example 161 is similar to the chord changes for **Billy Strayhorn's "Take the 'A' Train."**

Note:

1) The solo starts with a nod to a section riff from the original song and then cascades down in **tritones** on the D7(♭5) in bars 3 and 4.
2) The G whole tone riff in bar 6 sets up the stuttered line at the end of the first A section.
3) The second A section starts with a two-and-a-half-octave C major arpeggio and scale combo that ends up on the most important note of the D7(♭5) chord (A♭).
4) From bars 12 to 16, there is a great emphasis put on the **whole tone chords** [D7(♭5) and G7(♯5)], and very little attention is paid to the Dm7 and Cmaj7.
5) The B section starts with a **Lydian sequence** on the Fmaj7(♯11) chord.
6) There is a lot of **whole tone** material over the A♭7(♭5) in bars 21 and 22 that continues over the G7(♯5) in bar 23 and finally sets up a sequential riff that is carried over into the last A section. There is another whole tone sequence in bars 27 and 28 (check out the fingerings).

Solo #13

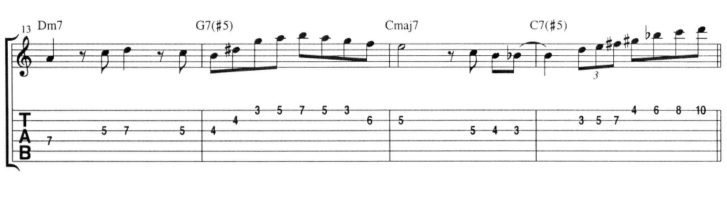

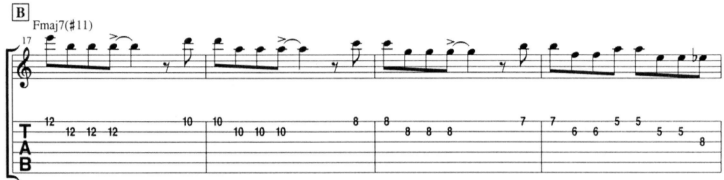

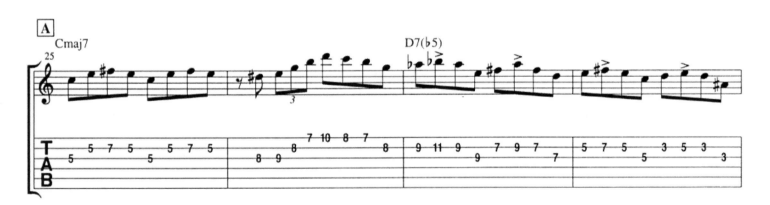

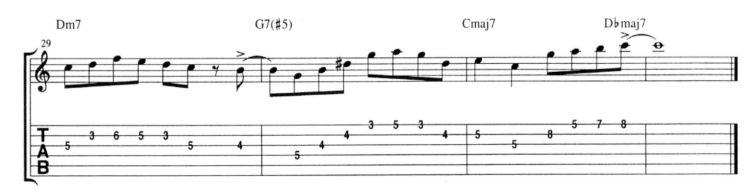

Summary Solo #14

CD 47 **Example 162** is loosely based on the chord changes to **Duke Ellington's "In a Sentimental Mood."**

Note:

1) The A section starts with a sequence that moves with the descending bass line. This is followed in bar 4 with a series of small riffs with the payoff in bar 8. There is a sequence similar to the opening one in bar 9. The bottom note (A) moves down chromatically and ends on the 3rd (F#) of the D9 chord in bar 11.

2) The A section ends with some whole tone lines in bars 12, 14, and 16.

3) The B section starts with a classic move on the D♭maj7 chord and a straight-up B♭ **Aeolian** run on the six chord (B♭m7). The same type of rhythmic and melodic soloing continues up to bar 22 where it gets a little weird. The first thing that happens here is that we have a three-beat-long riff in a 4/4 time signature, so we get a **polyrhythmic** feel happening. The second thing is that we have a string of **augmented chords** [B♭7(#5), E♭7(#5), A♭7(#5)] which allows the melody to creep up by half steps across the bar line. The effect is kind of cool.

4) In bar 25, there is a big descending **diatonic sequence** that reverses on the A♭7(#5) in bar 28 and ascends in triplets to a small quote of the melody.

5) The closing riff is a sequence that descends by a half step, ending on the major 7 (C#) and #11 (G#) of the Dmaj7 chord. Taking the minor tonic chord at the end of a piece and making it major is called a **Picardy third.**

Solo #14

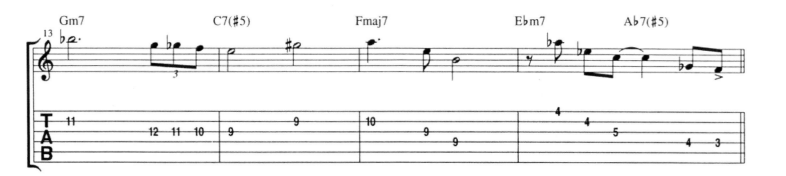

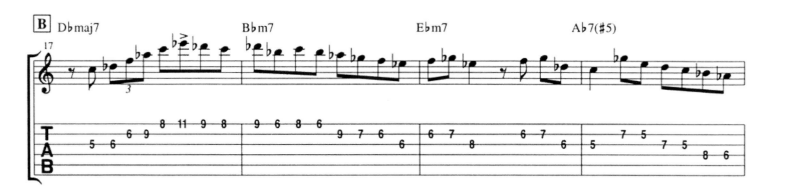

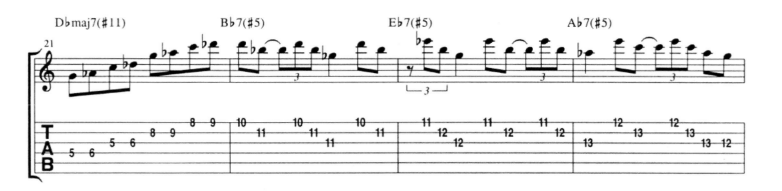

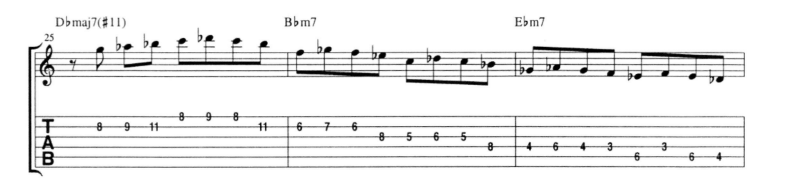

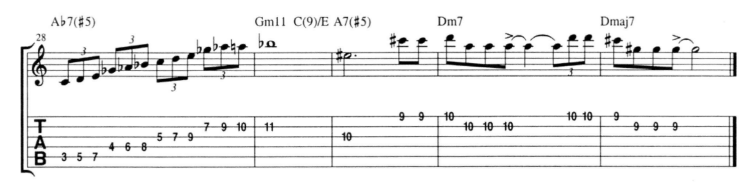

CHAPTER EIGHT:
Diminished Scale

The diminished scale is *not* one of the seven Greek modes. It is an eight-note scale. There are two different diminished scales: the whole step/half step and the half step/whole step. These scales are symmetrical, meaning they are a repeating pattern of intervals. The scale that I like to use is the half/whole diminished scale. This is because I look at all diminished chords as some kind of dominant 7(♭9) chord. By looking at diminished chords this way, it allows you to have a wide variety of options other than just the diminished scale. You can also blow over almost any type of chord with a diminished scale by going to its V7 chord and playing on that. This may seem a little far-fetched or hard to comprehend, but as you go through this chapter, it will (I hope) become clearer.

The arrangement of whole and half steps in the half/whole diminished scale is H-W-H-W-H-W-H-W.

Example 163 shows an F half/whole diminished scale in 1st position. There is no key signature for the F diminished scale.

Example 164 shows the F diminished scale played in every position across the fingerboard using four-notes per string (mostly). Slide your first finger to accommodate the first two notes on a string (when there are four notes). Notice that in every position, I start with the root (F). This is to reinforce the half/whole diminished sound.

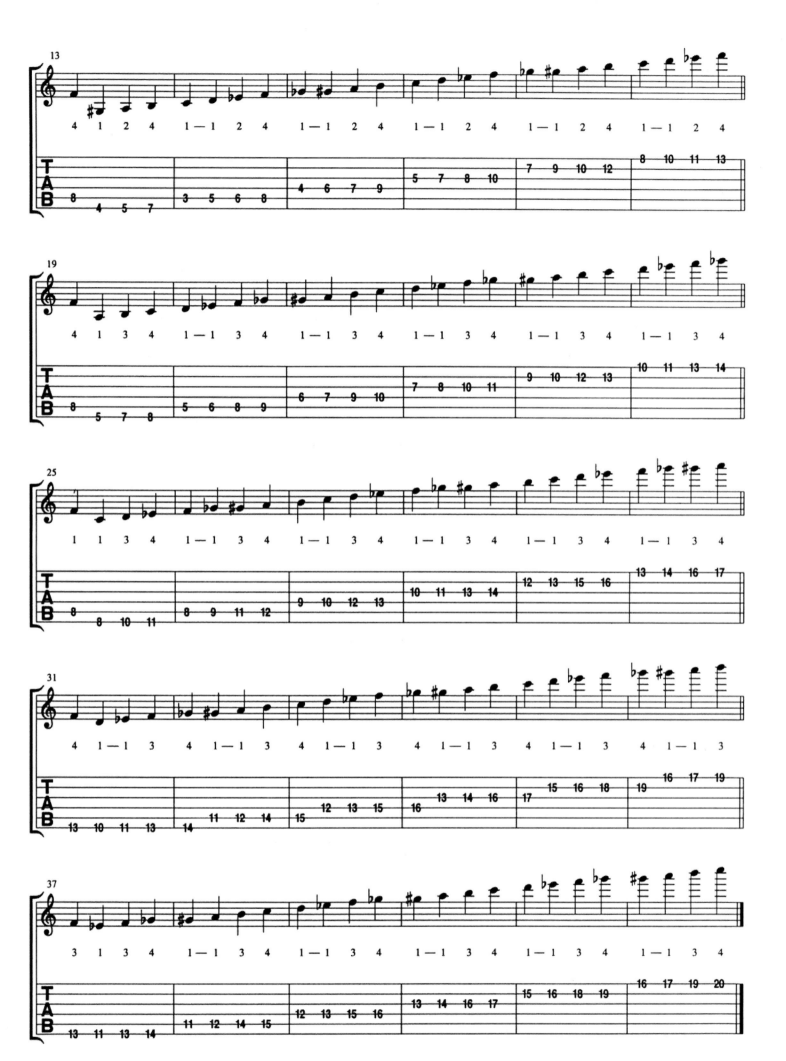

Diminished Scale

Example 165 shows some additional fingerings for the F diminished scale. Take all of these and come up with fingerings that work for you and fit your hand.

Diminished Scale Riffs

CD

48A

Example 166 is a line that I've heard played by saxophone players such as **Michael Brecker** and **Bob Berg** as well as guitar players such as **Mike Stern.** This is more like a bebop, and later a post-bop, type of riff because many of the symmetrical scales became these players' bread and butter. The line itself is just basically the **F half/whole diminished scale** over a G♭ diminished chord, which is really a substitute for, or an inversion of, the following dominant 7(♭9) chords without the root: A♭7(♭9), B7(♭9), D7(♭9), F7(♭9). I used F diminished because I related the G♭dim7 to the F7♭9 chord. The riff starts on beat 2, and there is a little turn in bar 2. Notice that the fingering is different going up and coming down.

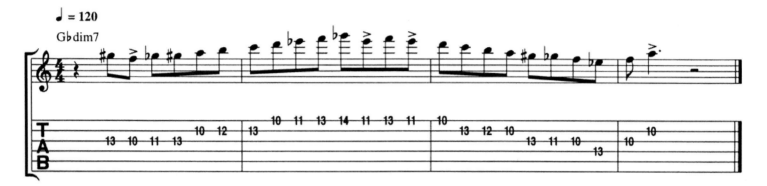

CD
48B

Example 167 is a short repeating phrase that shifts position in bar 3 and does a longer payoff in bar 4.

CD

48C

Example 168 gets pretty chromatic. This riff uses both the half/whole and whole/half diminished scales to form a **chromatically ascending line** in bars 1 and 2. Bar 3 starts with a low sax style "honk" (inserting a low root) and then proceeds down the F half/whole diminished scale.

Diminished 7 Chords

Example 169 contains some diminished chord voicings. I did not include the inversions because on guitar the fingerings stay the same. Diminished chords are four notes stacked in minor thirds. If you move any diminished chord up a minor third, you have its next inversion. Just do this four times and you have all the inversions for that particular diminished chord.

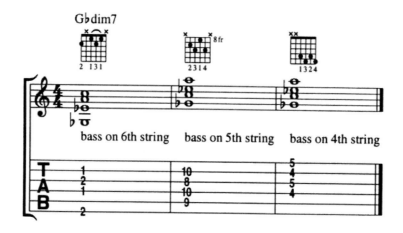

Examples 170 and 171 are some diminished 7 chord riffs. **Example 171** is the old tie-Nellie-to-the-train-tracks riff. If you ever play an outdoor gig by a train station and you notice a young lady tied to the tracks, just play this riff and help will soon arrive. It's also a good tremolo picking exercise. **Example 171** is a **Wes Montgomery**-style **syncopated rhythm** using the G♭dim7 chord and its inversions on the 5th and 4th strings.

Dominant 7(♭9) Chords

Here we will start to see the connection between the diminished chord and the dominant 7(♭9) chords. The half/whole diminished scale will work well on these chords, giving you the root, ♭9, ♯9, 3, ♯4, 5, 6, and ♭7.

Example 172 contains some fingerings for the F7(♭9) chord. It's plain to see that most of these inversions look like diminished chords. They are **inversions of the F7(♭9) with the root (F) missing.** The root is missing because, on guitar, we are limited by the number of strings and the shape of our hands as to how many notes we can grab. As we add more upper extensions to the chord, we tend to lose some of the fundamental chord tones. It's usually the 5th that you let go first (unless it's an altered five chord), but in this case it's the root that is let go. You will notice, though, that in the root position chords, sometimes the 5th was let go.

Dominant 7(♭9) Chord Riffs

CD
50A **Example 173** is a short rhythmic phrase that shifts its position within the bar. In bar 4 there is a ♯9 (G♯) added.

CD
50B **Example 174** is a riff that keeps the same note on top. In this case, it's the ♭9 (G♭). The line is also punctuated in bars 2 and 4 by the root (F).

CD
50C **Example 175** is a Latin-style riff. There is a syncopated lower note that alternates between the 5th (C) and the root (F). This simulates the bass player. The upper voices fill in the spaces between the lower notes, creating a counter-rhythm.

Dominant 13(♭9) Chords

Example 176 contains some fingerings for the F13(♭9) chord. By checking out these fingerings, you will see that the dominant 13(♭9) is a polychord. **There is a D major triad lurking in this chord.** The spelling looks a little weird because instead of F♯ there is a G♭ (D, G♭, A instead of D, F♯, A). I indicated voicings with the ♭9, 3rd, 5th, and ♭7th in the bass. I've tried to make these fingerings as practical as possible.

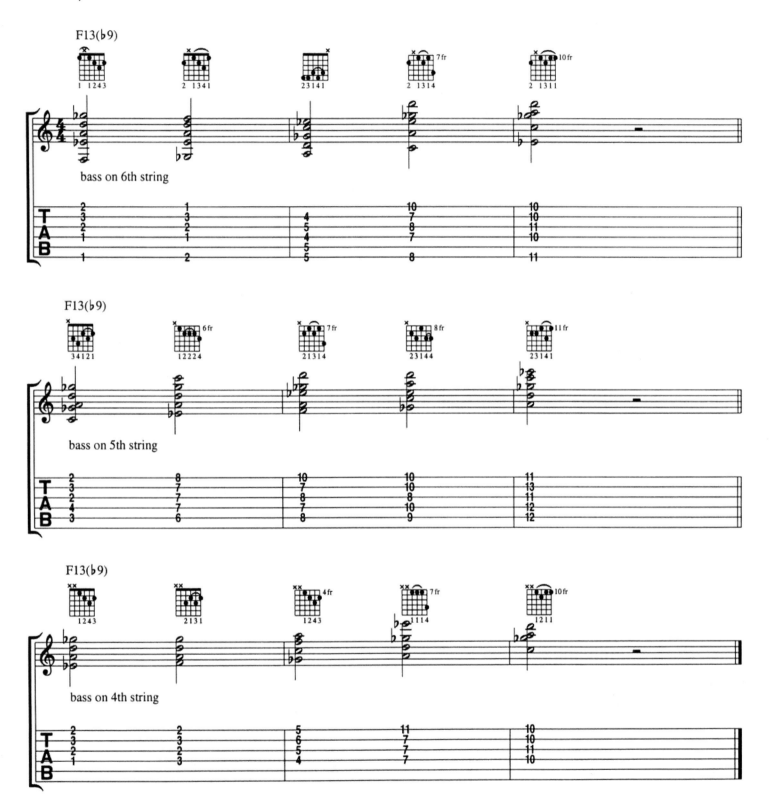

Dominant 13(♭9) Chord Riffs

Example 177 leaves a lot of space between the chord hits. Sometimes it's what you don't play that is most important.

Example 178 is a rhythmically smoother riff. In bar 3, I added the natural 9 (G) as an upper neighbor to the ♭9 (G♭).

Example 179 shows the F13(♭9) chord being used over a pedal note (F). Pedaling the root of a dominant chord and putting cool voicings on top of it is a great way to build tension in a song.

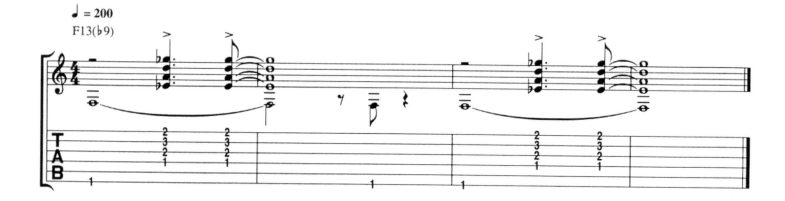

Diminished 7 Arpeggios

I am going to use the G♭dim7 arpeggio as the example for this section. You should think of this as an F7(♭9) arpeggio without the root.

Example 180 shows some fingerings for the G♭dim7 arpeggio. I did not repeat fingerings above the 12th fret.

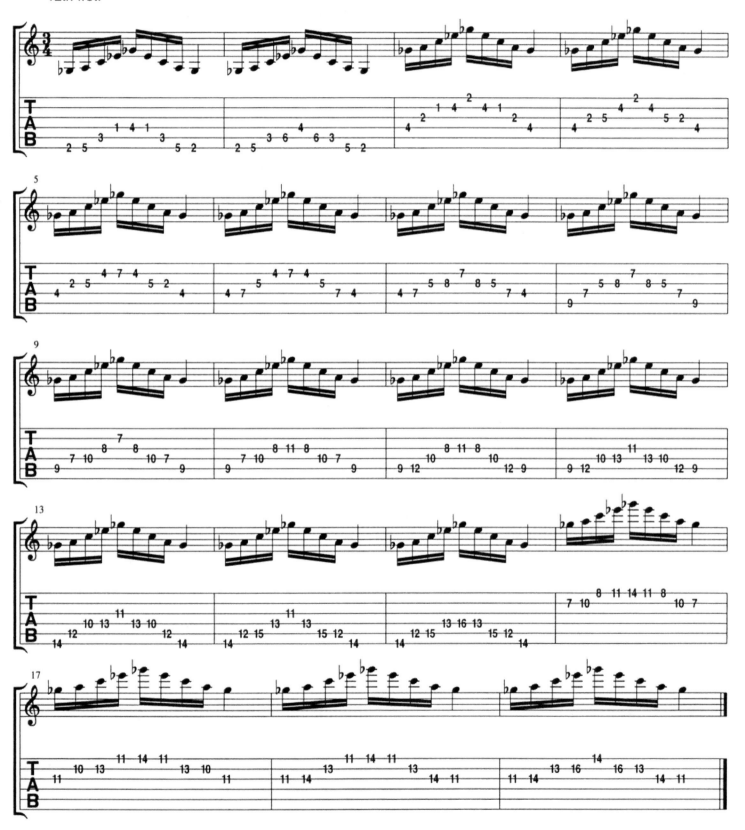

Now take these arpeggios and add the note F to make them F7(♭9) arpeggios.

123

Diminished 7 and Dominant 7(♭9) Arpeggio Riffs

CD
52A **Example 181** is over a G♭dim7 chord. This is a simple but effective diminished riff in the **Django Reinhardt** style.

CD
52B **Example 182** is a classic phrase used by numerous players over an F7(♭9) chord. Notice the rhythmic **push across the bar line** that propels this riff.

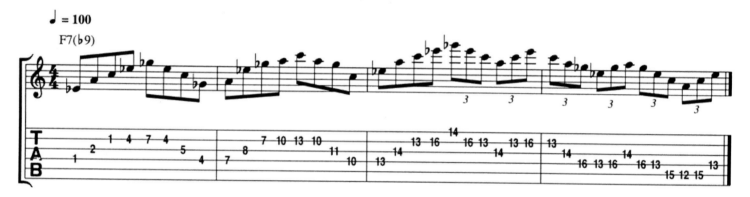

CD
52C **Example 183** is a two-part sequential riff. The first two bars walk up the F7(♭9) arpeggio in a rhythmic pattern and segue into the sequence for bars 3 and 4. The riff gets rhythmically dense as the bars progress.

Summary Solo #15

CD **53** **Example 184** is based on chord changes similar to **Rodgers and Hart's "Bewitched."**

Note:

1) The first A section starts with an **ostinato pattern** with the lower note ascending. The lower ascending line reflects the root movement of the chord changes. "Playing the changes" in this manner really helps your solo mesh with the song, as opposed to generic "hip" lines that could have been played over a variety of songs.

2) The first A section ends with a closing line lifted from **Lullaby of Birdland** that sets up the second A section.

3) Bar 9 starts with a low C honk—again, a technique that helps "nail" the root movement. This type of melodic technique can be traced back to **J. S. Bach.**

4) Bars 9 and 10 use a repetitive sequence (triplet followed by descending eighth notes). Sequences add strength and continuity to your solos.

5) Notice that in the second A section, I have replaced all the diminished chords with dominant 7(♭9) chords. This opens up the solo possibilities.

6) Bar 14 has a displaced octave C major diatonic riff that ends on the B natural (♯11) of the Fmaj7(♯11) chord in bar 15. The second A section closes out with a iim7-V7(♯5) riff into the temporary key of D minor (the saddest of all keys).

8) The last A section starts out with a similar theme to the first A section, except the notes are played faster. The song ends on another sort of classic diatonic riff but with some surprise chords in bars 31 and 32.

Solo #15

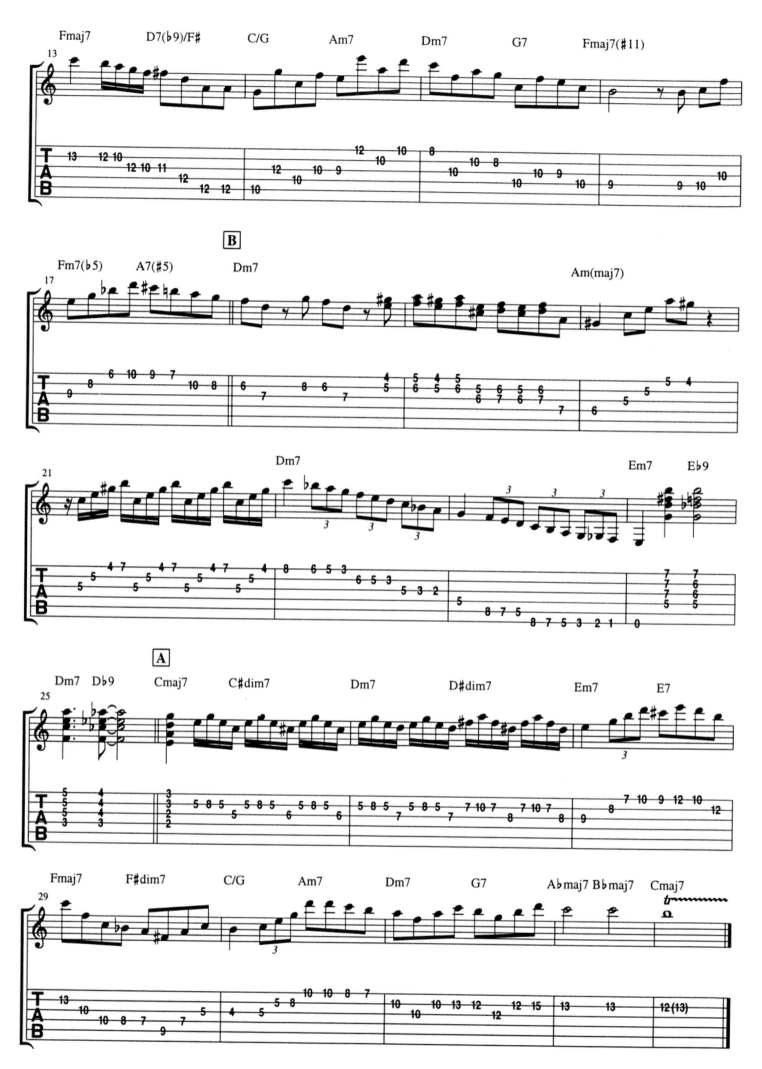

Summary Solo #16

Example 185 is similar to the chord changes in the **Duke Ellington** song, **"Caravan."** It should be noted that this song is in cut time. There is a "two feel" to each bar. The eighth notes do not swing.

Note:

1) The first A section starts with a half/whole diminished run up and down the C7♭9.

2) Bar 5 continues with the same scale but in a different sequence. Bars 9 and 10 give a quick nod to the melody of "Caravan" and then descend to an ending riff on the Fm7 chord.

3) The B section starts with a quote from the theme to the '70s TV show, "Barney Miller." (What can I say? It just happened.)

4) Bar 20 starts a sequence with the four triads found in the B♭ half/whole diminished scale (B♭, E, G, and D♭). In bar 25 the triads start to move in whole steps with a resolution to the F note (6th) on the A♭maj7 chord.

5) Bars 29 and 30 are diatonic except for the A natural chromatic passing note.

6) Bars 31 and 32 get pretty chromatic, setting up a series of quarter-note triplets in the last A section.

7) Starting on bar 39, there is a series of half/whole diminished runs that concludes on the root of the F chord with a couple of octaves thrown in for good measure.

Solo #16

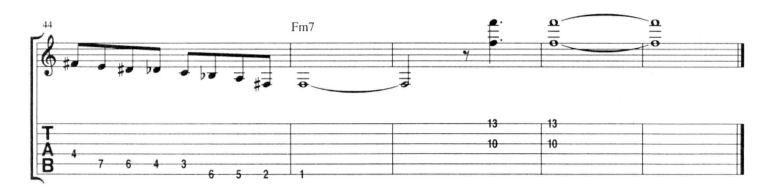

APPENDIX
Chord Harmony and
Guitar Chord Fingerings

In this book, we will be looking at different chord types: major, minor, dominant 7, and so on. Most of the chords presented are built in 3rds (1, 3, 5, 7, etc., from a related scale). On guitar, we cannot always finger these chords in numerical order (1 - 3 - 5 - 7). The guitaristic ways of fingering chords are described in the chapters throughout this book. I am going to take a minute here to show you a structured method for understanding chord harmony and fingering that you can translate to the guitar.

Triads and Inversions

Any chord can be "voiced" with any chord tone as its lowest note. There are three possible bass notes for any triad:

Root in bass: Root Position
3rd in bass: 1st Inversion
5th in bass: 2nd Inversion

Example 1 shows a G major triad with the bass notes on the 6th string in root position (G in the bass), 1st inversion (B in the bass), 2nd inversion (D in the bass), and root position one octave higher. (This will come in handy when we convert these to 7th chords.) Fingerings are indicated at the top of each chord grid, and chord tones are indicated at the bottom.

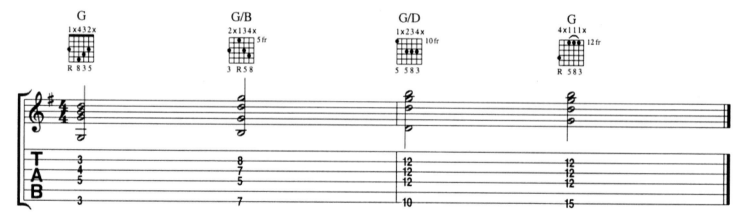

Example 2 shows a C major triad with the bass notes on the 5th string in root position (C in the bass), 1st inversion (E in the bass), and 2nd inversion (G in the bass).

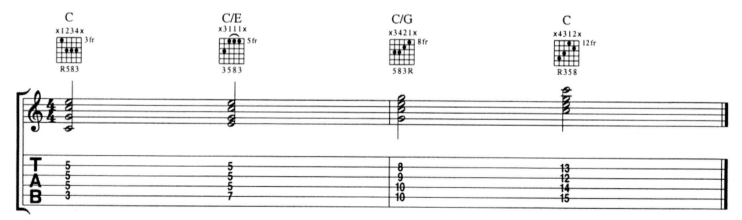

Example 3 shows an F major triad with the bass notes on the 4th string in root position (F in the bass), 1st inversion (A in the bass), and 2nd inversion (C in the bass).

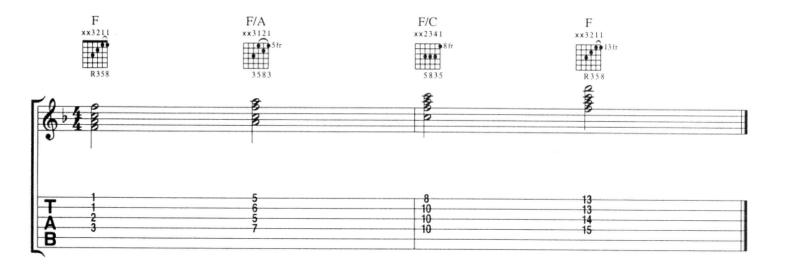

Example 4 shows how, by changing one note, we convert the root position G major chord to minor, diminished, and augmented.

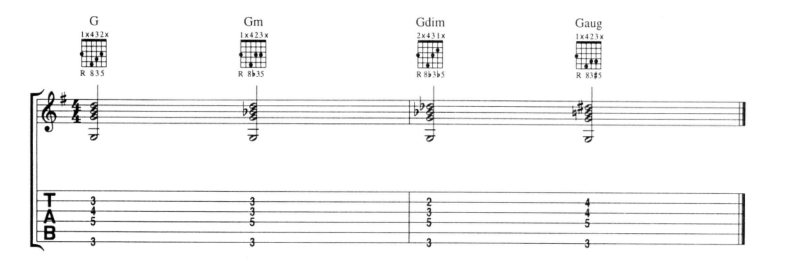

> Now convert all of the previous major chord fingerings to:
> 1) minor - flat the 3rd
> 2) diminished - flat the 3rd and 5th
> 3) augmented - raise the 5th

Four-Note Chords and Inversions

Let's continue this systematic approach and add the 7th to our major triad, making a major 7 chord.
There are now four possible notes to have in the bass:

       Root in bass: Root Position

       3rd in bass: 1st Inversion

       5th in bass: 2nd Inversion

       7th in bass: 3rd Inversion

Example 5 shows a G major 7 with the bass notes on the 6th string in root position (G in the bass), 1st inversion (B in the bass), 2nd inversion (D in the bass), and 3rd inversion (F♯ in the bass).

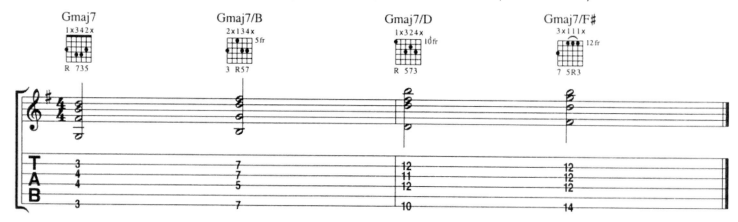

Example 6 shows a C major 7 with the bass notes on the 5th string in root position (C in the bass), 1st inversion (E in the bass), 2nd inversion (G in the bass), and 3rd inversion (B in the bass).

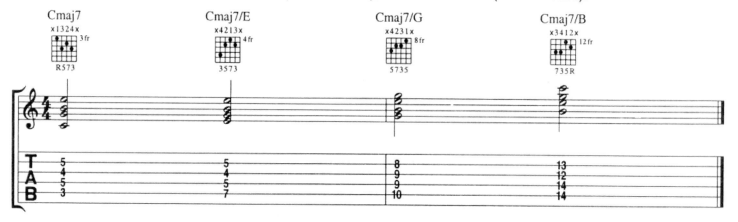

Example 7 shows an F major 7 with the bass notes on the 4th string in root position (F in the bass), 1st inversion (A in the bass), 2nd inversion (C in the bass), and 3rd inversion (E in the bass).

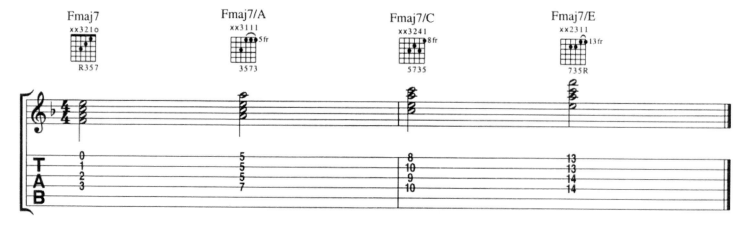

Example 8 shows how, by changing one note at a time, we can convert the root position G major chord to major 7, dominant 7, and major 6.

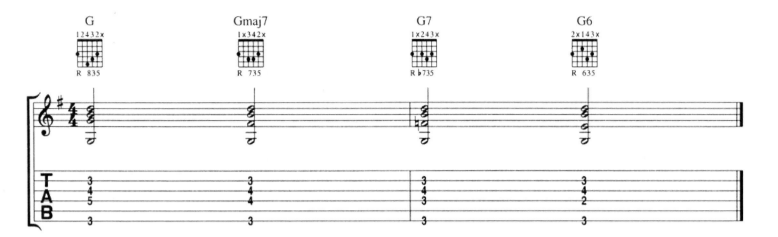

Example 9 shows how, by changing one note at a time, we can convert the root position C major chord to major 7, dominant and major 6.

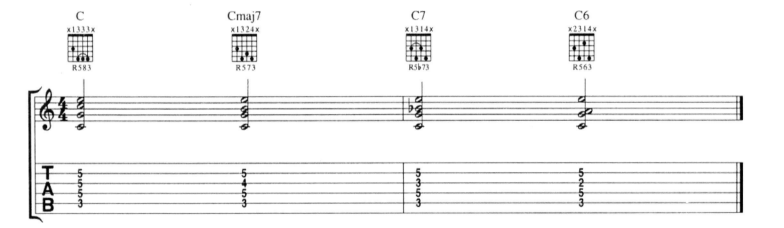

Now convert all of the previous chord fingerings as follows:
1) Major–Major 7–Dominant 7–Major 6 (drop the octave [8] by half steps: 8–7–♭7–6)
2) Minor–Minor(maj7)–Minor 7–Minor 6 (flat the 3rd, then drop the octave as in the previous example)
3) Minor 7(♭5) (half diminished) (flat the 3rd, 5th, and 7th)
4) Diminished 7 (fully diminished) (flat the 3rd, 5th, and double flat the 7th)
5) Augmented major 7 (raise the 5th)
6) Augmented 7 (raise the 5th of the dominant 7)
7) Dominant ♭5 (flat the 5th of the dominant 7)

If you know the function of each chord tone you are playing, making alterations is easy.

About the Author

Doug Munro is a critically acclaimed New York jazz guitarist. He has released numerous albums as a leader and has toured the United States and Europe promoting his recordings as well as doing clinics and residencies. Doug has recorded with Lew Soloff, Adam Nussbaum, Bob Berg, Wil Calhoun, Harvie Swartz, Danny Gottlieb, Will Lee, and Alex Foster. All of Doug's records were produced by award-winning producer Joe Ferry.

Doug is also an award-winning producer, composer, and arranger having worked with the biggest names in jazz, blues, and R&B. He has two NAIRD awards for R&B Record of the Year and Best Reggae Album of the Year for his arranging and production work on *People Get Ready: A Tribute to Curtis Mayfield* and the Skatilites' thirtieth anniversary album, *Hi-Bop Ska.* He also has two Grammy nominations for Best Reggae Album for his work with the Skatilites on their last two records, *Hi-Bop Ska* and *Greetings From Skamania.* In addition, Doug did orchestration work for the soundtrack recording from the movie *When We Were Kings,* which won an Oscar for Best Documentary Film in 1997.

As an educator, Doug created and heads the Jazz Studies Program at The Conservatory at Purchase College with a faculty that includes Steve Khan, Todd Coolman, Jon Faddis, and many other top jazz performers. Doug has a jazz instructional video, *Improvisation: Jazz and the Blues,* on Homespun Tapes.

Doug Munro endorses and thanks Dave Flores at Carvin, Bob Archigian at La Bella Strings, Tyne Rogers at Tech 21, Kim Keller and all the people at Kaman music for their Ovation steel and nylon string guitars, and Jimmy Archey at Gibson.

Additional information is available at Doug's Web site: http://www.purchase.edu/munro/.

Doug Munro Discography

As Leader:

- *Courageous Cats* (Novus Records)
- *When Dolphins Fly* (Optimism Records)
- *Autumn in Blue* (CMG Records)
- *The Blue Lady* (CMG Records)
- *Shootin' Pool at Leo's* (CMG Records)

As Arranger and/or Orchestrator, Producer:

- *We Remember Pastorius* (EMI Records)
- *The Soul of R&B,* Vol. #1: Billy Vera and Nona Hendryx (Shanachie Records)
- *The Soul of R&B,* Vol. #2: Chuck Jackson and Cissy Houston (Shanachie Records)
- *The Soul of R&B,* Vol. #3: Darlene Love and Lani Groves (Shanachie Records)
- *People Get Ready: A Tribute to Curtis Mayfield* (Shanachie Records)
- *The Soul of R&B Revue: Live at the Lonestar Roadhouse* (Shanachie Records)
- *Back to the Streets: Celebrating the Music of Don Covay* (Shanachie Records)
- *Bluesiana Hot Sauce* (Shanachie Records)
- *Hi-Bop Ska:* The Skatilites (Shanachie Records)
- *Bluesiana Hurricane* (Shanachie Records)
- *Greetings From Skamania:* The Skatilites (Shanachie Records)
- *When We Were Kings:* Soundtrack Recording (Polygram Records)
- *Skandalous Alstars: Hit Me* (Shanachie Records)
- *Skallelujah* (Big Music)
- *Love, Fun and Grief:* Various Artists (Big Music)

Video:

- *The Soul of R&B Revue: Live at the Lonestar Roadhouse* (Shanachie Records); executive producer and musical director
- *Jazz/Blues Improvisation* (Homespun Tapes); featured artist, instructional video
- *The Art of the Electric Bass:* David C. Gross (Homespun Tapes); performer and technical advisor

The 21ˢᵗ Century Guitar Method

The most fun, complete guitar method available!

 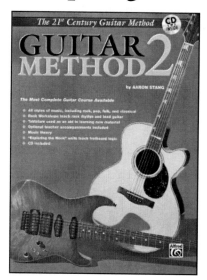 

Guitar Method, Levels 1–3: These are the three core method books. Together they comprise a complete guitar course covering a wide variety of musical styles—chords, theory, tablature, blues, rock, folk, classical, and fingerstyle! It's all here. Each book is available with and without a CD.

- All styles of music
- Rock Workshops teach rock rhythm and lead guitar
- Tablature used as an aid in learning new material
- Optional teacher accompaniments included
- Available with and without play-along CDs
- Now available on DVD (EL03842DVD)

For each level, supplementary books are available:

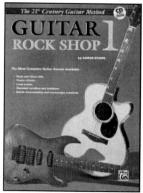  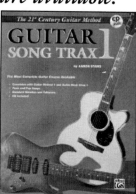  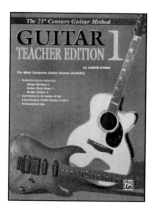

Rock Shop, 1–3:	***Theory, 1–3:***	***Song Trax, 1–3:***	***Ensemble, 1–3:***	***Teacher Edition, 1–2:***
A complete rock guitar method based on the blues. CD included.	A fill-in style workbook correlated to the core Guitar Method series.	Classic pop and rock songs with a play-along CD included.	Three parts plus optional bass, drums, and piano. CD available.	Breaks down every book in Levels 1 and 2 into 24 lesson plans each.